Maverick's Guide to Poker

One thing Pappy told me was, "If you know poker, you know people; and if you know people, you got the whole dang world lined up in your sights." There's enough sense in that to make the game worth all the trouble it can get you into.

—Bret Maverick

Charles E. Tuttle Company, Inc.
Boston • Rutland, Vermont • Tokyo

Originally published by DELL as *Poker According to Maverick*
© Warner Bros. 1962
Revised edition 1994 © Warner Bros. 1994

Published by the Charles E. Tuttle Company, Inc.
of Rutland, Vermont & Tokyo, Japan with editorial
offices at 153 Milk Street, Boston, Massachusetts 02109.

First Printing 1994
ISBN 0-8048-3032-0

Printed in the United States of America

Contents

Foreword

I've wandered around the West and up and down the Mississippi for many years, playing poker and having many an adventure. And through all these times, through all the notoriety I may have achieved, through all the games of draw and stud, I had one mission—the exploitation of my fellow man's ignorance of the laws of probability.

This may sound lamentably anti-social, but poker is and always has been a way of harmlessly expressing man's most deep-rooted anti-social drives. Knowing this about your fellow players is one of the vital secrets of good poker.

But for me, poker is more than exploitation of another man's ignorance of the odds. In some ways, it's a never-ending fascination at man's constant attempts at bucking the odds—mostly to my good fortune. This fascination was both a way of life and my way of making a living. Like my Pappy always used to say, "work is all right for killin' time, but it's a shaky way to make a livin'."

And while watching people buck the odds may have been fascinating, I never forgot the reason I was at that poker table. Like my Pappy said: "It isn't how you play the game, it's winnin' that counts."

But when all was said and done, my philosophy always came back to the most important advice my Pappy gave us boys—me and my brother Bart—when we left home—"you can fool some of the people all of the time and all of the people some of the time and those are very good odds."

In other words, even though I played poker for a living, it would be wrong to think of me as a gambler. Poker is the only game of chance I'll play, because poker, for me or any expert, is not a matter of chance or luck. This would be untrue if it were not for the fact that almost all poker players are gamblers. The man who plays odds instead of hunches can always count on winning in the long run.

So if you are interested in the fine art of poker-playing as a game of skill, patience, and animal cunning, you'll not only enjoy this book—you'll profit from it.

—Bret Maverick

Chapter 1

Is Poker a Game of Luck?

The way some men play it, I guess you'd have to admit that poker is a luck game—and all bad luck at that. I've met these fellows in every bar from here to Dodge City and back. They are losers by nature and by choice, because if they've got what it takes to master the simple laws of the game—which sometimes they haven't—they are too danged lazy or conceited or scared to play by 'em.

What I mean is, there are certain things you do in poker, and certain things you don't do, which, if you stick with them, sooner or later will earn you a stake. The losers don't understand this. So they get lazy and don't bother to learn the laws, or they take such a shine to themselves that they figure the laws don't apply to them. Or they're so scared of losing that they forget how the laws work. With a big pot on the table, buck fever has beaten more poker players than three ladies ever did.

But whether it's sloth, vanity, or purely fear, it all adds up to bad luck—the way the losers tell it. I never argue with these boys. They're liable to get mad and quit playing with me. And that would take a big bite out of the good luck I've been running with all these years.

Now, I tell you that poker, excepting with wild cards, is strictly *not* a game of luck—not for winners, that is. Winning poker players, over the long haul, must be experts with five weapons: skill, courage, strategy, psychology—and patience.

I can prove that this is true, and, if you follow the advice in this book, you'll not only have a lot more fun playing, but you just might fatten your bankroll a bit. Doesn't matter what stakes you play, either. Table stakes or penny ante, the laws are the same.

Most poker players like small-stake games, ranging from twenty-five or fifty-cent up to a dollar–five dollar limit. These players will gladly risk twenty to fifty to a hundred bucks in a game on the theory that, even if they lose it all, they can have more fun than they could bouncing around the town. And maybe get off cheaper, too.

There are plenty of players, though, who like high-stakes games. The laws of good poker were written by the winners of these games, and they are among the fairest laws ever passed. They apply to rich and poor alike, to strong and weak, young and old—everywhere in the world regardless of race, creed, color, sex, or previous condition. One of the hardest lessons the low-stake player must learn is that the laws of good poker, which came out of all the high-stake games ever played, apply equally to him. A chip may be worth a penny or a hundred dollars—the cards don't know the difference. It's no easier to win back a quarter in a quarter-half game than it is to pick up a C-note at pot limit.

I've been playing this game of poker for quite a spell now, having learned it with brother Bart practically on Pappy's knee. When my brother and I were no higher than his tooled-leather belt, Pappy took us into an El Paso saloon.

They were playing Twenty-One, Red Dog, Wheel of Chance, Faro—everything but poker. Pappy made a gesture that took in the whole place and said, "Boys, take a good look. This is what's known as gamblin'. Stay away from it. In games like this you haven't got a chance. Remember as long as you live—stick to poker!"

I got the idea then that he didn't consider poker a game of luck, but later he straightened me out on that. He said it wasn't a game of luck as long as I played with average players—who make up about 98 percent of the poker fraternity. "But if you ever get into a game with men who play as smart as you do, quit," Pappy once told me. "That's gamblin'!"

With all of Pappy's advice, I still had to learn the hard way that hope is no substitute for a full house. At the start, I was what Pappy called strictly a "run o' the herd" player—winning a little, losing a little, glad to stay about even.

After a while, I began to notice that certain pokes won in more games than they lost in, and I asked Pappy about it.

"No trick at all," he told me. "They're waitin' for good hands, sure enough, and then milkin' 'em for every dollar they're worth.

"That's the secret. Wait, wait, and wait some more until a fightin' hand shows up. Then if it's a big one, underplay it; if it's second-rate, overplay it. That's all there is to it, exceptin' one thing: every once in a while mix it up, to keep wise guys like me from catchin' on."

Bart and me took Pappy's advice to heart. We sat in a steady game and kept accurate tally on a thousand hands, dealt to an average of seven players over a period of weeks. Straight stud, five cards, and nothing wild. In such a game, we found that about twenty-five hands can be dealt every hour. In a ten-hour session, that's about two hundred and fifty hands, or about four sessions for the thousand hands we kept track of.

In two of those four sessions, my record shows that I lost because I held a lot of "second best" stuff. Good fighting hands, all right, but I was nosed out of the money by something slightly better. In the other two games, though, I won enough to take care of my losses—and then some.

During the next few years, I found myself leaving the poker table with more money than I started with in three out of five games. And this winning percentage has increased ever since. It's all in Pappy's simple trick of watchful waiting, of getting out quick with the losing hands, and of making the fighting hands pay off the most.

I don't worry too much about hands that come out second best. More often than not, if I've "overplayed" them correctly, second-rate hands will drive potential winners out. If they don't, I stand to lose a little. But I make that up by trapping the pigeons with a real winner I've "underplayed" properly. And staying out of pots I know I can't win helps keep the balance in my favor.

The art of overplaying and underplaying your fighting hands is really the art of the actor. That's the acceptable name for it. Really it's the art of the con man, the swindler, the seller of snake oil, or—where I come from—the horse thief. (If you can't call a spade a spade at the poker table, where in the world can you?)

I figure anything short of cheating goes in a poker game. I remember one time when I got roped in to serving on a jury. The sheriff came in to break up the game and take us all over to the court house. I showed him my hand and said plaintively, "Can't it wait for this, sheriff?"

The sheriff glanced at the hand, which was a busted straight, nodded blankly, and said, "Well . . . finish the hand, but make it quick."

I threw in a medium-sized bet (too large a one would have been disastrous) and everyone folded.

The successful poker player must be able to create an illusion as to the strength or weakness of his hand, whether by casual remarks, manner of betting, facial expression, or by other devious means. Poker faces come in all styles, grim and gay, sour and smiley, rigid and relaxed. Your own personality will dictate the mask you pick for each occasion, the mannerisms you cultivate to lasso your particular lambs. But you must cultivate them—or end up a loser.

Your mask and your manner don't affect the laws of poker, of course. That's one thing you've got to remember. It's the man across the table you want to fool—not yourself. So stick to the rules of sound play, whatever role you assume for each of the thousands of poker hands you'll play in your lifetime.

The first of these rules is that when you lose a big pot, or a whole slew of pots—don't stampede. I've seen some men driven near loco finishing second in two-man pots for an hour at a time. They didn't just look desperate, they were desperate. And when you're desperate, you just can't play right. You start yearning to get even, and that desire builds up in you till it starts crowding out your common sense. That's when you begin drawing for inside straights, and when you do that you might as well saddle up and ride, because nothing good is going to happen to you where you are.

Even seasoned poker players have trouble learning to smile when their three Jacks lose to three Queens across the table—especially when they had the side-winder figured for two pair all the time. If you're an amateur, it may comfort you to know that when things like that happen even old-timers swear off the game. (It's easy to quit playing poker; some veterans have done it hundreds of times.) But somehow they always come back—and so will you—to ambush the cuss who stung them with those three Queens. They will lure this fellow into reading their hand for a bluffing bust, only to dry-gulch him with an Ace-high flush. There is no greater pleasure on earth than pocketing the proceeds of such a duel.

Whether you win or lose a particular hand on any particular night, the art of creating illusion is still one of the most important factors in successful poker. I will never forget Matthew Wicker, who ran the bank in Crystal River and was a master at this sort of thing. When I was just about saddle-broke, Matt and I bucked each other in many a game, and I guess he was one of the toughest players I ever tangled with.

His face was trained finer than frog's hair. Depending on his strategy, it would glow or glower so hard that it was impossible to discover in it a clue as to the strength of his hand. His method of betting was equally confusing. But to top it all, every time he won—which was often—he would deliver a silver-tongued lecture to the losers on how they should have played their hands.

The strange thing was that, though these lectures were intended only to add to the confusion of his opponents, they were delivered so soberly and sincerely that these unfortunate folk listened intently, and followed his advice. When it failed to deliver the desired results, Matt merely improvised credible reasons, and added a few new hints for the dudes' future play. Since he was a consistent winner, what could they do but follow his suggestions? It was a vicious cycle—for everyone but Matt.

I sat through a few of Matt's lectures myself before I caught on to his game, and then I began to keep score on him. Although he looked as if he played a loose game, I noticed that he almost never stayed in any stud hand unless either his hole card or the first open card was equal to or greater than any other card showing.

He didn't need a pair wired—just high fighting cards with not more than one of them showing in other hands. If there was no raise, he would stay for a third card.

If this card paired him, or gave him high card, he immediately got tough, and, if in the right position, raised the limit.

Matt's object was to get as many players as possible to fold. Most players, including many old-timers, don't see how smart this move is. The average player who is sure he's high man on the third card will call timidly, hoping all hands will stay to build the pot for him. But if you make it easy to stay in the game, you encourage your opponents—regardless of whether they hold weaker or stronger hands than yours—to hang on and possibly beat you.

This theory was proved to me twice over in a game I watched one night in the bunkhouse. On the first round of betting in five-card draw, everybody dropped out but two Swede homesteaders, who had been invited over for a fleecing. They raised like crazy for a while and then they each drew one card. While the crowd of pop-eyed punchers looked on, the Swedes raised each other again until there were several hundred dollars in the pot.

Finally one said, "I call. Vat you got, Ole?"

"Qveens," Ole said.

"How many qveens?"

Ole held up a finger. "Vun."

The other Swede sighed and shook his head. "By yimminy, you sure lucky tonight, Ole! You vin again."

Ever since then—and it's been a long time now—I've wasted no time driving out the chore boys who haven't got enough to beat me on the board—if I can. If I can't, then I know I've got a fight on my hands, and that's when poker really gets to be fun.

About the same time Matt Wicker was operating in Crystal River, there was a judge—Sam Scott was his name—over in Dawson. He made quite a name for himself playing poker in the back room of the Sundown Saloon on Saturday nights. All week long, Sam would be handing out time to ornery cowhands who had broken chairs rassling at the bar or had maybe set the town on its ear with a little mischievous gunplay. Come Saturday, there was nothing he liked to do better than settle down for a night-long poker session that usually ran until time for church.

One reason he liked the game so much was that he almost always won. I can still hear him chuckle pleasantly as he raked in pot after pot with monotonous regularity.

After playing in several such sessions, a neighboring rancher, who was no slouch himself, told the judge, "There's no denyin' it, you're just the luckiest player in the world!"

Judge Sam turned deadly serious. "Friend," he said, "there ain't no such thing as luck in poker—I mean no such thing as luck stayin' continuously with one player in game after game. And I can prove it.

"If you want," he continued, "all seven of us will meet next week, and we'll deal out a thousand hands—all cards face up, five cards to a hand and no betting. We'll keep count of the winner of each hand. And I'll offer anyone a two-to-one bet that every player in the game gets about the same number of winning hands!"

No one took him up on the wager. But Bart and I tried the experiment later, and the judge was right.

I thought about this for a long time. In every game I had played in, there always had been one or two players who seemed luckier than the others. But the experiment proved that luck didn't stay consistently with any one player.

What makes players *seem* lucky is their ability to play the game smartly when they have short runs of good luck, and to know when they have better than an even chance to win.

For a spell of about five years, I played with a group of hands in a friendly game maybe once a week. It was a real educational experience.

In order to get seven players together regularly, we had to have at least fifteen on tap. Some dropped out temporarily because of losses, others because their foremen thought they ought to get out on the range a little more often, or something like that.

After a time, it was clear that out of the fifteen, only four or five would wind up winners over a period of a year. The rest lost in game after game and, at the end of any given year, their losses were sizeable. Invariably, they blamed it on bad luck.

It just wasn't so. Every one of them had the same number of potential winning hands, over a period of time, as any of the actual winners had.

What made them lose was impatience. They just wouldn't fold their poor hands, and they spent countless chips trying to outdraw better ones.

The consistent winners had an iron rule that kept them from bucking their heads against this stone wall.

It's a rule as simple as ABC, and the player who sticks to it can't help coming out ahead. Here it is, in Pappy's golden prose:

"He's got 'em and I've got 'em to git."

All it means is that if a player in a stud game has a higher hand than yours showing, turn your hand down and wait for another.

For instance, suppose you have a Jack in the hole and another showing. You have raised the high-card opener and met his re-raise. On the third card, an opposing player, with a Queen showing, catches another Queen. With two more cards to be dealt, you are beaten on the table then and there, and you must fold the Jacks immediately.

The theory behind folding your Jacks at this point is that the pair of Queens has as much chance

13

as you have of improving on the next card. Sure enough, I vary this rule from time to time. If a review of all hands reveals there are two more Queens out and no other Jacks showing, as in the picture, you have about a one-in-five chance of beating the Queens with a fake raise, providing you have a King or an Ace showing to make the raise look good.

In a game with better-than-average players, at

Jack in the hole

14

least two or three will drop immediately. If you catch a third Jack, the pot is almost surely yours, because you know your opponent can't get a third Queen. Ordinarily, the best he can hope for is two pair; it's a hundred-to-one against his making a full house.

Most conservative players, however, would turn down the Jacks the moment the second Queen showed up. They rarely buck the obvious odds. When they succeed in bucking the odds, though (and they don't even try unless they have sound reasons), they avoid one trap that has snared thousands of unsuspecting greenhorns—and that is the belief that lightning can strike many times in the same place.

Take the case of the loose player who stays for the third Jack, catches it, and wins. Unless he steels himself to resist temptation, he will try the same strategy again and again, and it will cost him pot after pot. If you stick with the odds, day in, night out, you will win more in the big pots, lose less in the small ones. And you will actually increase your chances of winning when—if the wind is right—you abandon caution and buck the odds regardless. Your occasional foray into loose play will catch your opponents off guard, and they will fear you far more than they should.

There was one player in this game of ours named Dudley Jones. In a friendly sort of way, some of us called him "Generous" Jones, though mostly we were satisfied to use his regular moniker, "Dud." He was a middle-aged sheepman who ran a big spread not too far from town, and the game was something he looked forward to after a week of windburn and saddle sores. He went into each hand like a kid digging into a bag of candy, and almost invariably he called all bets right through the fifth card.

Obviously, he outdrew better hands quite often, but, because the law of averages is unbreakable, he wound up a heavy loser in every game for months on end. We liked having old Dud around.

This continued for almost a year. Then, one night, Dud came up with a streak of winning hands and nearly broke up the game.

Although he left the table that night with practically all the money, he did not come near making up his earlier losses. But, worse than that, his experience convinced him that loose play actually paid off, and his later losses doubled.

A player like this is as welcome as a panful of gold to a prospector.

When I am sure of such a player's style, I wait for good or even average hands, and then raise the daylights out of him. This generally reduces the number of players in any given hand, and leaves the patsy to me alone. In nine out of ten such duels I have to win, because I wouldn't be in the play unless I had him beaten at the start.

"Generous" Jones should be a caution to all players, tenderfoot and veteran alike. It is a great temptation to toss chips into the pot for "just one more card." It takes a lot more nerve to fold a hand full of high cards (but no pairs) when a pair is show-ing on the board.

But if you want to win, you must train yourself to do just that. There is no doubt that you will make enemies that way, especially among the losers, but in the end even your enemies will grow to respect you.

Furthermore, there is no satisfaction greater than being a winner. The feel of blood-bought "plus" money in your jeans is a lift that only a poker player knows.

A loose player may win an occasional game, just as a dude may land a lucky punch in a drag-out fist fight with a careless cowpoke. But over a period of time, both must lose.

Some of my poker-playing sidekicks have asked me, "What do you get out of playing poker when you stay out of so many hands?"

I tell them, "I play to win—the object of the game. If I can't win according to the odds, I turn my hand down and wait for another. I figure that's money in the bank—*your* money in *my* bank."

The average player finds this philosophy difficult to understand. He wants action and plenty of it, and believes that the only way he can get it is by throwing money into a pot.

Occasionally, a player will ask, "Suppose everybody in the game played them close to the vest like that? We'd all turn down almost every hand, except the high man."

The answer is that they would not, and do not. As a general rule I avoid games in which I am equally matched. But there was an occasion two years back when my lovely and larcenous friend Annabelle Bransford staked me to a game with six of the toughest poker players west of the Mississippi. (It turned out that Annabelle had her own devious reasons for arranging the game, but that's another story!) While it lasted, this was the greatest game I'd ever played in, for with seven solid players the game comes into its own as a battle of wits. I won a goodly sum, but a large part of it was pure luck.

In a game like that, each hand is an adventure to be remembered. The highlight of such an evening is to catch a cautious player with his stirrups loose and beat him with a losing hand. There need be no big winners or losers to make such a game exciting.

Good players can be talked into folding top hands just because other good players raise them. Each player, having respect for all the others, may be bulldozed into retiring a good hand if someone really tangles with him.

In such a game, psychology is king. Nothing amuses (or enrages) a tenderfoot more than calling poker a game of psychology. But, of course, that's just what it is.

Psychology has been defined as "the science of the human mind and its operations." Pappy had another was of putting it:

"Poker is civilized bushwhackin'!"

"When a player raises with no pairs showing and you have a pair with your hole card," Pappy used to say, "you ask yourself how is that hombre thinkin'? Has he got hisself a better pair, or is he tryin' to make me hightail it out of here?"

In a situation like that you must make a quick decision. You must decide whether to test him once with a re-raise or to call him and wait for another card, or to fold your hand.

That's what makes poker a game of wits and courage—and fun besides.

Most people are fighting a never-ending battle to prove that they can whip something. Poker is one way of having a showdown with destiny without someone getting killed—necessarily.

Chapter 2

Some History and
Some Rules of the Game

This book is written for the man who understands poker, but who doesn't understand why he loses so often to players who aren't as good as he is. I figure you are pretty familiar with the basic dos and don'ts; in other words, that you have a basic knowledge of the game. Still, a brief look at the history and rules may be in order, especially for those who haven't played in a while or who may be thinking about taking it up for the first time.

The history of poker is difficult to trace. It started, probably, with the French game "Poque" and the old Persian card game "As Nas." The English "Brag" and the French "Ambique" are kin to poker, and they in turn are supposed to have borrowed from the older Italian game of "Primiera." In any case, the gypsies are entitled to some of the credit. They were great gamblers, who, in their wanderings, brought many card games from the East during the fifteenth century.

But poker, as it is played now, is as American as the Rocky Mountains. It started in New Orleans among sailors who made a two-syllable word out of the French "Poque." "Poque" was played with a 32-card deck, with three cards making a hand. "As Nas" used a five-card hand, but an entirely different deck. During the early 1800s poker was adapted to a 20-card deck with Aces and court cards. The 52-card pack came later.

The first variety was straight poker, or bluff. It was closed poker with no draw. A buckhorn-handled knife, or "buck," was placed on the table to indicate the man who was to ante. This was passed to the left as the game progressed—hence the phrase "passing the buck." The earliest type of poker was showdown. Stud, the draw, straights, flushes and many modifications that we know today were added as time went on.

Some History and Some Rules of the Game

Poker traveled from New Orleans on the Mississippi steamboats. It was played mostly by Fancy Dans in checkered vests and beaver hats who took on all comers and were pretty quick with a queer deck. Stakes were high in those games, with plantations, slaves, blooded horses, and large sums changing hands many times.

As the West opened up, and the rush began for California and Klondike gold, poker spread to the mining camps and the boom-town saloons. Those who played it were held in contempt by the pious, and some still think the game is not quite suitable for the parlor. There were those, however, who learned to respect it as a minor science, and who played it artistically. Henry Clay, Daniel Webster, and other great Americans were among these men and their head-to-head contests have made history.

Poker not only has elements of science and art, but also contains the elements of luck and courage. As such, it combines many of the factors that make up the lives of every man. Because it reproduces life in miniature, it has become one of the most popular games ever played.

It certainly had become a part of our language. We all know what a poker face is; we call for a showdown; we have an Ace in the hole; we pass the buck; we suspect a man of being a four-flusher; and eventually we all cash in our chips. This in one measure of how well poker imitates life—and vice versa.

Throughout the world the game is now played according to the rules developed in America, and it has become highly respectable. Its fans will tell you it provides the ultimate test of brains, willpower, and guts. As such, it is truly a man's game—rightfully earning the skillful player a place of honor among gentlemen.

Unlike other card games, poker has few hard and fast rules. Certain rules are used almost everywhere, but others vary from town to town, and even from game to game. In the late 1800s, attempts were made to standardize poker, but nobody ever succeeded in doing it—then or since. The game grew fast, and the rule book never caught up with it.

"Local options" give the game some strange twists. There is the famous story of the tenderfoot who got into a fast game in Virginia City way back when. He found himself holding a royal flush, and bet the limit. He got plenty of action from a gray-bearded miner but, smelling a rat, he merely called the last bet instead of raising. The gray-beard showed a pair of deuces, a four, a five, and a six, and raked in the pot. The newcomer's indignant protests were useless.

"I held an Old Cat," the miner said, pointing to

a sign on the wall, which read:

AN OLD CAT BEATS ANYTHING

The tenderfoot took it like a man. Seven and a half hours later, he found himself holding a pair of deuces, with a four, a five, and a six. He bet all he had and, at the call, laid down his hand in triumph. The miner, who had a pair of Aces reached for the chips.

"Not so fast!" the tenderfoot shouted. "I've got an Old Cat!"

"Too bad," the miner said, pointing to another sign on the wall. It read:

AN OLD CAT
IS GOOD ONLY ONCE A NIGHT

That story may sound a little crazy—and it is— but there are local options that aren't too much different. There are combinations called Big Cat, Little Cat, The Dog, The Tiger, The Kilter, and The Skeet, and a lot of others; they are really "nothing" hands with an artificial value. For instance, The Big Tiger runs eight to King, with no pair. It beats a straight, but not a flush. The Little Dog runs two to seven, with no pair; it beats a straight, but loses to a Big

Tiger. That will give you some idea.

We're not going to spend time on that kind of foolishness. Luckily, there is some agreement on the fundamental rules of standard draw and stud—and they form the basic code of the game of poker as it should be played. However, there is a confusion on one basic rule in stud that remains to this day, and I learned about it the hard way—at a cost of sixteen thousand dollars.

It happened on the momentous occasion on which I first met Annabelle. We were on the Memphis Queen heading for New Orleans, and Annabelle had been lying back, waiting for me to develop a straight in a five-stud hand. I finally did, although it developed accidentally. I was playing my hole card, an Ace, and came up with a straight. Annabelle's high card was a Jack, no pairs showing, no possibility for a flush. The highest she could have had was a pair, but she kept raising me. I turned over my straight and Annabelle turned a pair of nines. And she won!

Using the ship's copy of Hoyle, which she had insisted from the start was to rule the play, she showed all of us at the table the clearly written rule that "straights are not played in stud poker unless it is agreed to recognize them at the start of the game." Some "Hoyle" books of today still carry this rule, and the reason is obvious: straights in five-card stud will generally be the result of accident, and often of poor playing.

Rank of the Cards

The value of the cards in poker runs in ascending order from the two (or deuce) through the ten, Jack, Queen, King, and Ace. The Ace is normally high, but for purposes of forming a straight (see below) it may be considered low. Thus Ace, two, three, four, five is the lowest possible straight, while in a ten, Jack, Queen, King, Ace straight, the Ace is high.

Rank of the Hands

A poker hand consists of five cards, and only five. There are many hands in poker—some of them winning hands—in which the cards bear no significant relationship to one another. The significant relationship among the cards in poker hands lies in whether they match other cards in face value, or in suit, or follow in the sequence of their rank, all in certain combinations that have been assigned values according to the difficulty of achieving them.

The lowest-rated hand containing cards with such value is ONE PAIR, which contains two cards of equal face value, and three cards having no significant relationship to each other or to the pair. One pair is the lowest in the scale of rated hands, simply because it is the easiest to get.

Next in rank is TWO PAIR, a hand containing two different pairs, plus one odd card.

Next highest is THREE OF A KIND, that is, three cards matching in face value, plus two cards unrelated to each other or to the triplets.

A STRAIGHT is next highest, and is made up of five cards in the order of their rank, but not all of the same suit.

Next is a FLUSH, which combines five cards of the same suit, but not in the sequence of their rank.

A FULL HOUSE is next in line, and is made up of a pair and three of a kind.

FOUR OF A KIND—four cards matching in face value (with an odd card, of course)—is next highest.

The highest hand of all is a STRAIGHT FLUSH, which consists of five cards in sequence of their rank and all in the same suit. An Ace-high straight flush is called a ROYAL FLUSH, and cannot be beaten in a non-wild card game.

The winner of the hand is the one, among those who have called all bets, who holds the hand of the highest rank. Thus, any straight flush beats any four of a kind; any four of a kind beats any full house; any full house beats any flush; and so on down the line.

Some History and Some Rules of the Game

One Pair

Two Pair

Three of a Kind

Straight

Flush

Full House

Four of a Kind

Straight Flush

29

If two players hold hands of the same rank, here is how the winner is determined:

1. In straight flushes and straights, the man whose top card is higher takes the pot. In flushes, if they both have the same high card, the pot goes to the man whose next highest card tops his opponent's. Ties are broken in this manner down to the fifth card, if necessary. If a tie still exists, or where both players have a straight flush or a straight and the same high card, it is a Mexican standoff, and the players split the chips.

In no case is a poker hand ever determined by a ranking of suits. All suits rank equally in determining winning hands in poker. (In casinos that force the low-card to open, the suits are ranked in alphabetical order: clubs, diamonds, hearts, spades. Therefore, a deuce of clubs is considered lower than a deuce of diamonds when determining the opener.)

2. Holders of four of a kind, three of a kind, and one pair are separated by the rank of the combination they hold, the pot going to the holder of the higher four, three, or pair. Thus, four tens beats four sevens, three Kings beats three eights, a pair of Aces beats a pair of Queens, and so on. If two players hold one pair of the same rank, top man is the one with the highest ranking odd card; or, if they are

equal, the next highest odd card, and so on.

3. In full houses, the winner is the man whose three of a kind is the higher.

4. In two-pair hands, the winner is the man who holds the highest pair. If these are equal, the second pair in each hand decides. If both pairs are of the same rank, the odd card decides. Here again, five cards of identical rank is a standoff, and the players split.

Now let's get back to those hands in which the cards have no significant relationship to one another. There's more of this kind than any other, so naturally it ranks lowest. It doesn't even contain one pair, let alone a significant sequence or combination of cards of the same suit.

Hands like these, especially under expert handling in five-card stud, can still be winners. In the event that two players remain in the pot with such hands, the winner is the one whose top card is highest. If they are equal, the second highest card in each hand decides, and so on. Again, if the hands are identical as to rank, it's a dead heat and they halve the pot.

A word of caution for the amateur about straights: while the Ace may be counted either high or low, it is always either the first or last card in the sequence. There are thus only ten possible straight combinations: Ace through 5, 2-6, 3-7, 4-8, 5-9, 6-10, 7-J, 8-Q, 9-K, and 10-Ace. A straight cannot "turn the corner," which would put the Ace in the middle of a sequence as in J-Q-K-A-2. This is not a legal straight, because in any straight containing the Ace, it must either be the high card or the low.

You may notice that every one of the ten straight combinations contains either a five or a ten. This is a small point to remember when playing any form of stud poker. If you see fives and tens a-plenty exposed on the board, the chances of players not holding them making a straight are reduced considerably, no matter how threatening their cards may look.

Wild Cards

Real poker is played according to the rules I've just outlined. Even die-hards are sometimes trapped into games in which certain cards are tagged "wild"—which means that they can be counted as any card the holder wants them to.

The most commonly designated wild cards are the four deuces, and the two one-eyed Jacks—the Jack of hearts and the Jack of spades. Sometimes, the single one-eyed King (the King of hearts, also called the Suicide King, due to the position of his sword) gets the call. But no card can be wild in any game unless the dealer calls it before he starts distributing the cards.

The reason wild cards were introduced to the game was to make good hands show up more often. For this reason, identical hands that contain wild cards usually are considered lower than "natural" hands of the same rank. For instance, in two identical straights, the hand with the fewest wild cards would be considered the winner. But this is not always the rule. If you become involved in such a game, make sure you know the house rules before you start to play.

Chapter 3

Ten Commandments
for Poker Players

There are, maybe, a hundred rules for sound poker that, if followed, will make you a winner. One of the old saws is: never play with a man with the name of a city in his name, or anyone named "Slim" or "Doc." This rule probably was started by amateurs who got their wallets emptied by a more experienced player, or with Doc Holliday. Since I've beaten many guys named Slim and Doc—including Holliday—I can't quite see the logic in this rule.

But the commandments listed below are

absolute musts. If you can make yourself stick to them, and not go chasing false scents over strange trails, they will work for you faithfully like the old plow-horses they are.

1. If you don't have a fighting hand, drop it and wait for another.
2. In five-card stud, never draw a third card unless your hole card or your open card either equals or tops the highest card showing around the table. (Unless you draw a pair on your first two cards, of course.)
3. In draw poker, "Jacks or better" to open, never call an opener unless you have the pair of Jacks beaten. (Exceptions will be pointed out later.)
4. Never draw to an inside straight.
5. Never draw to a three-card flush.
6. Always call a known bluffer if you have better than an average hand.
7. Don't play poker with women.
8. Don't play with players who can't afford to lose.
9. Don't play yourself if you can't afford to lose.
10. If you find yourself in a losing streak, relax and wait! There will always be another hand or even another game.

The first commandment may seem simple and easy to follow, but the average player usually has to fight against himself to do so. That's because he craves continuous action and, as the game goes on, his fever increases to the point where he may lose all sense of proportion.

The key to success is PATIENCE.

If you can't develop patience, you must lose—perhaps not in one game, or even in five, but eventually. Without that brake on your buckboard, you will leave the game with the deed to your Aunt Emily's chipmunk ranch in somebody else's wall safe.

Patience is the hardest thing for any poker player to develop, no matter how long he's been around. Turning down average hands to wait for good ones takes more guts than most men can muster. That's one reason why if you can do it, you'll end up a winner.

Personally, I like to play and lose for an hour or so. This gives me a chance to read the players, how they play their hands, and to pick up any "tells"—little quirks that a player unconsciously makes when he has a winning hand or is trying to bluff. This patience obviously costs me some money up front, but once I can read a player, once I can read their hands, I usually end up winning that money back and then some.

Just what to do in this long waiting period without going loco is a personal problem. A cup of coffee may help to settle your nerves, but don't try anything stronger. Even good players find it tough to overcome the effects of red-eye.

If you're an amateur drinker, be especially careful. I've seen sound players send a good game galley-west under the influence of alcohol—calling everything in sight with a pair of threes. One of the steadiest players I ever knew used to call for a shot whenever he hit a losing streak. After a couple of these, I've seen him stay for a third card with a deuce down and a four showing. Without the drinks, he would have been gone like the slug from a Colt .45. So, if you can't handle drinks, don't touch the stuff during a poker game. As my old Pappy told me when I left home: "Son, never touch hard liquor or hard work."

The second commandment is of the greatest importance, and is followed religiously be every cautious player. Remember that the man who holds a card higher than either of yours has exactly the same chance to improve as you have, and he pays no more for the next card than you do.

Naturally, the rule calls for variations and a close study of all open cards. If I'm beaten on the board, I will sometimes pay for one more card if neither of my cards is showing elsewhere, and if my opponent's higher card also appears in another hand. My chances of improving in this situation are slightly better than his. A little cautious gambling may be in order, especially if I have a good number of winning chips in front of me. If I try it at all, I might even go so far as to raise in an effort to move two or three players out of the competition. But, win or lose, it isn't the best poker, and shouldn't become a habit.

If I lose the hand, I make sure that everyone sees my hole card plain, just to prove what an awful sloppy player I can be.

If the going has been tough, though, I don't try it. The other players will sure as shooting read my raise as born of desperation, and will re-raise me to a fare-thee-well.

The third commandment is just another version of Pappy's principle: "He's got 'em and I've got 'em to git." The opener mathematically has just the same chance you have of improving his hand—and since he started ahead he's likely to finish that way.

Many old-time poker players, however, will vary this rule if they hold a four-card flush or a straight open at both ends, even though they know the odds are against them.

Here's where the good player really becomes an

actor. If he is the last man to call, he will raise the pot in an attempt to force out as many players as possible (doing it in such a way that the other players don't think he's raising just because no one else did, usually while holding chips throughout, as if he intended to use them when the bet came to him). The action that follows is what makes poker players come back time after time.

The character with the four-flush or four-card straight will toss in his odd cards and maybe say, "Just give me one more deuce!" He hopes to make his opponents believe he has two pairs, or is drawing to three of a kind and is holding a kicker.

If he fills in his flush or straight, he has better than an even chance of winning the pot. If he doesn't, he still has one desperate move left.

Naturally, he has watched carefully to see how many cards were drawn by each player and how the betting has proceeded. Suppose the opener checks and another player bets; the bluffer must quickly make up his mind on one of two courses of action. He must either fold—or raise. He can't possibly just call, because that would destroy the illusion of strength just as surely as folding would.

Don't try this super-fake if the other players know you are either a tenderfoot or a loose player. Some solid player is bound to call you—and beat you—with a pair. But if you are known as a cautious player, it can work and you may rake in the chips, making sure your victims see you won with a bust.

This bit of legal thievery may pay big dividends later, because the boys who got burned by your bluff will call your bets for hours. Since you don't make a habit of raising on four-card flushes or straights (remember, you're a cautious player), you will collect a heap of wampum when you reveal at the end that you really have the goods.

It may seem ridiculous to many readers of this book even to mention the warning in the fourth commandment. Maybe so. But if I had a dime for every player, even every reasonably good player, who tries to fill inside straights, I'd never have to work again—at poker or anything else.

At eleven-to-one, the odds against making the inside straight are just too darned big. There are only four cards in the deck that can do the job. In a seven-handed game, thirty-five cards already have been dealt, and the chances are that at least two, perhaps three, of those four cards are already in the other six hands.

Exactly the same principle applies to the fifth commandment.

Suppose you have three hearts. In a seven-hand-ed game, more than two-thirds of the deck will have been dealt at this point. This means that, on the average, more than two-thirds of the hearts are gone. Since there are only thirteen hearts in the deck and eight or nine are probably already out, you must gamble on catching two of the four or five remaining in the pack. You have about as much chance of that as you have of winning a pair of dice in a church raffle.

The sixth commandment is based on the fact that for some people, bluffing, like cattle rustling, becomes a bad habit—or worse, a serious mania. Perhaps early in their poker careers they won some outstanding hands that way, and can't get rid of the notion that the same thing will happen again—and again and again.

You can spot such a player easily. Though he will steal an occasional pot, he will lose many more than he wins. It is good poker—in an otherwise solid game—to call such a character time after time, if only to cure him of the habit. You will cure him in time, provided you call with enough in your hand to beat him.

The seventh commandment—well, you be the judge. Poker is a game of percentages in which skillful handling of the variable factors makes the difference between winners and losers. Since women are supposed to be expert in all forms of guile and cunning and are alleged to have powers of insight and intuition that are denied to men, you might think they'd make better poker players than men ever could. Unfortunately, this isn't the case.

There are good reasons why women can't stand the gaff at the poker table. One is that they have a different approach to the iron-clad restrictions imposed by both the rules of the game and the laws by which the odds operate. In everyday life, so many exceptions are made for women that they find it hard to believe these exceptions don't exist in poker. This discovery nettles them, causing them to pout, stamp their feet, or worse.

Another reason is that women find real poker too slow. They crave faster action, and wilder games than men are usually willing to play. They take the predictability—and therefore the science—out of the game, and make it a carnival instead. When the odds, and the science based on these odds, go down the flume, you just aren't playing poker anymore. You are playing seven-card blind man's buff.

But the biggest reason why women don't play good poker is that when they practice cunning they can't resist staying around to see how well it works. Women's curiosity is so overpowering that it is almost impossible to drive one of them out of a hand. The result is that while they occasionally win a big one, they lose much more often, forcing the men in the game to relieve them of much coin. This is a mean task for any man, but it's a pleasure compared with explaining why they can't have it back.

The eighth commandment presents a problem. A player who consistently comes into the game with "short money" is bound to be a loser. Eliminating him from the game is a difficult, but necessary task. If he has lost a lot he demands a chance to get even, and if you turn him down watch out for trouble.

The craziest story I ever heard about a "short money" player concerned Stuttering Smith, a top cow foreman, who had a weakness for both whiskey and poker. His boss, Tom Cardiff, thought so highly of him that he offered Stuttering a hundred head of beef if he'd quit the game for a year. They drove the trail herd into Abilene and Stuttering headed for the nearest honkytonk, to cut the dust and enjoy a sociable game.

His luck was phenomenal. When Tom looked in later he saw that Stuttering was loaded with chips. "Stuttering," he said reprovingly, "that ain't no way to keep our bargain."

"Go to bl-bl-blazes," Stuttering told him. "Come m-m-morning I'll b-b-b-buy you out, r-r-r-ranch and all."

Tom was so mad that he hopped the first train and started back for Texas. Pretty soon Stuttering's luck began to change. He couldn't win for losing, and pretty soon he was flat broke. A little later, another cowpoke found him outside with his arm around a telegraph pole, tapping on it with the handle of his six-shooter.

"What the devil you doing, Stuttering?" he asked.

Stuttering said, "I'm t-t-telegraphing T-t-tom C-c-cardiff for g-g-g-get-home m-m-money."

At the Sundown Saloon, we had a rule to take care of short money players. No player could lend or borrow money during the game, and no notes or checks or IOUs could be exchanged.

This rule was plenty tough sometimes on the boys whose markers were known to be as good as gold. But in most cases it worked; after a few games, the short money players usually stayed away. Maybe they know we were really doing them a favor, and maybe not. But we saved our game for those who could play without worrying about putting their homesteads on the line.

The same rule should apply to you, of course. If you haven't enough cash to see you through a losing streak, or if you can't afford to lose at all, stay away. Remember that the man who has the most money in his pocket can weather the storm best, and generally has the best chance of coming out on top, all other things being equal.

The short money man is psychologically beaten before he draws his first hand. He knows he can't afford to lose, and fear warps his play. He folds winning hands, and stays in losing ones.

Now, for the last commandment, you and I both know that there is no such thing as consistent luck in poker, that is, in luck staying with one player all the time. But every poker player also knows that there are such things as *temporary* winning and losing streaks. If you get caught in one of these losing streaks, there is only one way to beat it.

WAIT! And then wait some more.

Turn down your cards and keep turning them down until you see a bend in the road. Above all, don't toss chips into the pot on weak hands just to keep your morale up. You'll need those chips to ride the good hands real hard. When the fighting hands begin to show, bet big! If your opponents read desperation in this, so much the better. They'll give you a big play—and increase your chances of coming out even.

On the other hand, all good poker players respect their streaks. There are times when cards just seem to fall from heaven. When the cards seem to be coming your way, you must play these streaks just as hard as you can for as long as they last.

These streaks are not a license to play loose, but if the cards seem to favor you, you may consider staying for one more card when you'd normally drop. Plus, other players will respect your streak, which gives you a decided psychological advantage if you decide to bluff after a run of good hands.

There is an eleventh commandment, perhaps as important as the first ten, which should be second nature to any serious stud player: *Examine all your opponents' cards carefully and compare them with your own.*

For instance, if you have a high hole card and two of the same are showing across the table, your chances of catching the fourth are about as good as a pound of pure creamery butter on a boarding house table.

You might catch it, sure, in one hand or another. But don't hold your breath waiting for it. You'd have a better chance at a hanging.

There is one other commandment that I have heard other players include in this list: don't play poker with players who say they are playing for the first time. This commandment has two reasons behind it. The first reason contradicts everything I said about all poker luck being bad. The one exception is so-called beginner's luck. Beginner's luck sounds like a cliché, but I've seen it proved true time after time.

A cowhand once asked a group of us if he could sit in, admitting he'd never played before. After we explained the basics, he was only slightly nervous, but seemed to grasp the main ideas.

In one Jacks-or-better draw game, the new cowhand passed, meaning he didn't have a hand better than a pair of Jacks—we didn't figure him smart enough to sandbag. But after a first round of heavy betting, he was still in the game. Then he drew one card. We figured he was shooting for a straight or a flush—if he knew to do that much. He couldn't have held two pair, or he would have opened or at least checked rather than passed.

There was more spirited betting after the draw, and danged if he didn't call every bet. Those of us still in the pot figured him for a tenderfoot and a sure loser, especially since each time he called he looked pained, as if he'd just sat on a cactus. I had my Ace-high flush, so I wasn't concerned even if he had his straight or flush.

Sure enough, he won the pot with a full house. He had two pair at the start, but neither was higher than Jacks. He took "Jacks-or-better" literally, which fooled—or, more accurately—distracted everybody. And that's the point.

Beginners don't understand the rhythm of the game and can foul up your concentration. Their bets are illogical, if they can figure how much they have to put into the pot to begin with. Since the beginner I faced didn't raise, and since I knew he was a beginner, it was impossible to read him or his hand since it was impossible to know how much he knew or understood.

In some ways, beginner's luck isn't luck at all. They win because all the other players become frustrated to the point that they are dragged down to the beginner's poor playing level.

The second reason behind this commandment is that not everyone is who they say they are. Many a slick player has gone into a game feigning ignorance. All the other players lower their guards and, sure enough, lose their stakes to the "beginner."

The best rule: assume everyone knows exactly what they're doing, regardless of how they act or what they say.

Chapter 4

Poker Psychology— Or "Civilized Bushwhacking"

One of the biggest kicks in poker is getting inside the minds of your opponents, and using what you find there to beat them at their own game. That's why men who like and understand other people make the best players. It takes a lot of nerve to call a big raiser when you have a medium hand, but I have seen it done successfully thousands of times. In almost every case, the caller succeeded because he instinctively understood the motives of the raiser.

Maybe the raiser was a four-flusher at heart, though he tried to hide this from his friends. Maybe he was driven by a secret urge to win every hand, regardless of what he held. Maybe he had been a consistent loser and was trying to get even in just one hand. There are as many more "maybes," I reckon, as there are poker players.

Politicians usually make excellent players because they have to understand people to get ahead in their game. Big operators—the city bankers and the big-spread ranchers—also are pretty good, as a rule, and for the same reason. And watch out for dudes who have no regular means of support, but live by their wits. They are usually the best players of all.

Most poker players fall into certain categories that are fairly easy to spot. First, there's the cautious but ambitious man who makes a study of every small venture he goes into, even if it's just shoeing his horse. With experience to temper his judgment, he can be a top player.

Then there's the fellow who is trying to pay off the mortgage on his spread, the buckboard, the new barn, and still have enough left over for a few buttons and bows. Chances are this man will be over-cautious and turn down many winning hands.

And there is always the panty-waist who's

scared he'll cause someone trouble if he wins. When he has the top hand, this joker won't raise. In the end, he has to be a loser. His opponents with the strong hearts will take it all.

I've noticed that a good poker player generally is a success in whatever business or profession he's in, or he could be if he put his mind to it. Why? Because he understands people, and that's the foundation for success in this world.

In a poker game, the guy who rubs elbows with the world is a ten-to-one shot over the guy who burns the midnight oil sopping up book-learning. That goes double for poker-playing itself. Nothing you pick up from this book will take the place of squaring off with your opponents face-to-face.

Two of the most fascinating hands in the history of poker show how psychology—or "civilized bush-whacking"—is the governing factor in the game.

The first is told in *The Gentlemen's Handbook of Poker*, the first authoritative work on poker, published a long time ago. It concerns two of the greatest men in American history, Henry Clay and Daniel Webster, who were squared off in a no-limit game.

Webster dealt a hand of draw. Clay drew one card. Webster stood pat, and threw in a wad of cash. Clay raised, and Webster re-raised. More raises followed till there was $400 in the pot.

The two men studied each other. Clay thought he had had enough and called Webster's last raise.

Webster smiled wryly. "I've got a pair of deuces," he said.

"That beats Ace-high," said Clay. "You win."

These masters of psychology were both top-notch poker players. Being smart as foxes and twice as wily, each accurately figured that the other was bluffing. The result depended only on how long one or the other could hold out.

This hand has been argued over by poker experts for years. There are those who hold that Clay could have won if he'd had the guts to make one last big wager—say the size of the pot. Dan'l, with only a pair of deuces, might not have dared to call. I think they're right, but I wouldn't know for sure. I wasn't there. Others claim that Clay was a fool to call in the first place. They may be right, but they'll never know for sure. They weren't there either.

The second of these great hands will make more sense to the average player because it's a lot closer to home. It was played at the Sundown Saloon, and involved two legendary experts of the West—"Straights" Fowler of Tensleep, Wyoming, and Billy Dundee, the famous one-armed dealer from Laramie.

The game was draw, Jacks or better to open,

with a twenty-five dollar limit and a five-dollar ante. Fowler dealt, and Dundee opened under the gun. Jingo Bates raised quickly, and "Dirty" Potts, who ran the restaurant in town, called. "Straights" Fowler re-raised the limit. Dundee called without hesitation, but Bates dropped. Unexpectedly, Potts raised the limit at this point. Both Fowler and Dundee appeared surprised, but they called regardless.

This was a lot of action before the draw. But with Dundee and Fowler in the game, poker didn't start until the dealer called for cards to the players. Even with more than three hundred dollars in the pot, the boys hadn't started to sweat yet.

Dundee drew two cards. Potts stood pat. Fowler drew two himself.

The bet was checked to Potts, who bet the limit. Fowler raised, and Dundee re-raised. At this point, Potts folded his pat hand. Fowler raised once more, and looked inquiringly at Dundee. Dundee raised the bet, and Fowler bumped him again. Without batting an eye, Dundee dropped his hand.

"You've got a winner," he told Fowler. "Your four Kings beat me. And I'll bet even money your kicker is an Ace."

"Straights" Fowler was a mite peeved at having to pass up the chips he had expected from Dundee in answer to his last raise. But he was even more peeved over the fact that Dundee had called his hand to a "T." He laid down four Kings and an Ace, and asked for an explanation.

"Straights," Dundee said, "when Jingo raised my opening bet, I could figure him maybe for two pair or low triplets, like he was trying to drive us all out quick. When a solid citizen like you bumped him, though, I had to figure you for at least a pretty good set of threes. I had a good hand myself—three Queens—but with Aces and Kings out against me, all I could do was tag along and hope for the best.

"When Jingo folded, it meant my guess on his hand was sound. But I was rocked a little when Potts bumped. That sandbag hit me pretty hard.

"On the draw, though, I picked up the fourth Queen and an Ace. Unless the odds were going crazy, I had to figure I had Potts' pat hand beat, and probably yours, unless you were luckier than you deserve to be.

"I checked, expecting to wallop someone with the sandbag myself when the bet came around to me. I knew it had to because Potts couldn't check his pat hand into a pair of two-card draws and hope to fool anybody. Sure enough, Potts bet, and you raised. I knew you weren't bluffing because you had just called on Potts' last raise, so you must have improved some.

"I wasn't going to let you or Potts off the hook without a struggle, so naturally I bumped. Potts was in the middle between two raisers, and dropped. I figured then he had a straight or flush, which he knew just wouldn't stand the action.

"When you raised me again, I knew you had to have at least a full house, but my four ladies still looked good and I let you know it. Then you came back at me again. I figured it this way: You know me too well to think I'm bluffing in this situation, especially when I opened under the gun and called all bets until after the draw. Also you know that if I have 'em, I'll bet 'em all the way, which I did. So your last raise tells me you have a full house beat. That means four of a kind and no straight flush, since you drew two cards.

"Your four of a kind had to be high, because on my play you have to figure me for four of something, too. My Ace kicker tells me you haven't got four big ones, so it has to be Kings. But unless you hold an Ace yourself, you can't be sure that my fours aren't bigger than yours. Now you could have had that Ace before the draw and thrown it away, but in that case it was at least even money you'd have held it as a kicker and drawn one card to keep your three Kings hidden better. So it's at least even money that the kicker in your hand after the draw is an Ace.

"Since I know you held Kings, and four of them at that, my four Queens were no good, and there just wasn't no point in my wasting twenty-five more on 'em."

With all that money in the pot, and four Queens in your hand, wouldn't you have tossed in another twenty-five dollars? You probably would have. But to Dundee the old poker adage, "Never throw good money after bad," was second nature. Once he knew "Straights" Fowler had him beat, he threw in his hand without a whimper.

When you play poker, you're running a business—investing in the pots that look likely, and passing up the dogs. The cards may determine who has the high hand, but the man with the high hand isn't always the winner. That's what makes poker different from any other card game you can name. It's the only game in which a worthless hand can win it all, *if* you know how to do it. And it's the only game in which you can toss away a winner without even knowing it—if you get careless.

The reason is simple: poker is a two-gun game. The hand you hold in your left mitt is one gun, and the money you toss around with your right is another. They're both important, but the money is the equalizer. It can make a pair of deuces as strong as a straight—or stronger—if you know how to handle it.

This makes poker different from other card games in another way. You have control of your own destiny. In other games, the run of the cards may be sometimes lucky, sometimes not, just as it can be in poker. But, lucky or not, you have to play them the way they come.

In poker, nobody sticks a gun in your ear to force you into any pot, or out of it, either. You play or you don't play, and you're the only one who decides. Like I said, you're running a business, and if luck is bad you can minimize your losses. If luck is good, you can stretch your winnings. Since luck is evenly distributed over the long haul, the real difference between winners and losers lies in their ability to lay low during the slack periods, and to ride hell-for-leather during the booms. But to really do the job you've got to know more than just the cards and the odds. You've got to know the men you're up against, or they'll get the drop on you every time.

To play winning poker, you must accept the dog-eat-dog way of looking at things. Even the church deacon—if he ever plays—has got to connive with the rest of us at beating his fellow men out of a buck.

Now, the player who only stays in hands in which he has a cinch will eventually get no callers. His opponents will wise up to his game and turn down their hands. After a while, this man is bound to lose or die of pure loneliness.

The same goes in reverse for the player who bluffs all the time. At least one player will call him, and win. But if you vary your play—sometimes bluffing, sometimes riding a cinch, but mostly just playing it close—you're going to worry the best of them.

And here's where "civilized bushwhacking" comes in big. If the pace is fast and loose, you play loose, too. If there are one or more tight players, make sure you have the cards before you buck these fellows. In either case, vary your style of play from deal to deal, so that no one can recognize the value of your hand from the brand you give it.

Pappy tells this yarn about how too much consistency can cost you plenty. An old blacksmith and his son sat down to a game one night with some Eastern slickers. They had been warned to watch these dudes carefully because they looked smart enough to cheat.

Next day, one of his friends asked the son, "How'd you make out?"

Poker Psychology—or "Civilized Bushwacking"

"Pa and I lost the shop," the son said, "but, by God, they didn't cheat us! We called every hand!"

Chapter 5

How to Play Draw

Many old-timers believe that draw, often called closed poker, is the toughest game of all, not just because all the cards are concealed but because there are so many ways to cover your tracks by faking on the draw itself. The draw, and the betting that goes on before and after the draw, are your only clues to your opponents' hidden cards. Since these offer such opportunities for "civilized bushwhacking," really conservative players often seek out the more scientific game of five-card stud.

Let's take a look at how draw is played, and you can judge for yourself. After the first dealer has been selected by lot, the deal automatically proceeds around the table to the left. Each dealer in turn is expected to shuffle the cards thoroughly and this is mighty important, because cards will stick together in a poor shuffle.

The dealer offers the deck to the player on his right for a cut. In many games the cut is considered optional, but not where I come from. Sure, all the players are honest, but there is always the chance that someone may unwittingly get a flash look at the card on the bottom of the deck. The safe rule is to cut—always.

It is customary in most casual, low-stakes games, for each player to ante an agreed amount before the deal—generally one chip of the lowest value in the game. Under other rules, the dealer antes for everyone. In higher-stakes games, a pot is created only when a bet is made.

Being a percentage player, I am against the rule calling for anyone to ante. It's strictly unfair to players on a losing streak. I often play in games for hours on end without winning a hand, or even playing one, to study the play and the players. In a game in which I am forced to ante, I'd be forced to watch as my stack of chips dwindled anyhow—on antes alone.

The theory behind the all-around ante is that

with a good pile of chips in the pot to start with, the play will be livelier. Players with low hands will be tempted to put more chips in and draw cards. Now, that's where poker science goes down the well. When a losing player falls for this lure, it's a ten-to-one bet he will lose even more. The same goes for the ante by the dealer only, of course.

But the ante is popular and, as they say in Abilene, "You can't buck a whole herd of steers." After the ante, the dealer distributes five cards face down to each player, one at a time in turn clockwise.

The most popular draw game is Jackpots. No player can open the betting after the cards are dealt unless he had a pair of Jacks or better.

The privilege of opening goes to the first player to the left of the dealer and, if he passes, to the next player on the left, and so on until the pot is opened or the deal is passed around and a new one started. The first player has the option of passing, regardless of what he holds. If he has a strong hand, he might do just that to see where his opposition lies.

In poker lingo, this is called "passing under the gun." Sometimes it is a smart move, for if someone else opens the pot, the passer may merely call and be figured a lot weaker that he really is. I have seen old-time players pass under the gun while holding hands as high as three Aces. If someone else opens they will call "reluctantly," and not take over the driver's seat until after the draw. Even if they don't improve the three Aces, they have an excellent chance to win a big pot.

Don't follow this practice too often, however. Many a player loses a winning hand just because he won't open under the gun. Sometimes it's because no one else has the required Jacks or better; sometimes it's because his opponents smell a rat—and fold.

After the cards are dealt and the pot has been opened by someone with Jacks or better, the betting proceeds with each player in turn either meeting the bets of the preceding players, raising them, or folding his hand and withdrawing from the deal. The betting ends when every player remaining in the deal has bet the same amount. The smart player, of course, will watch every bet and every raise carefully because they are, up to this point, his only clues to what his opponents hold.

When the preliminary betting round is complete, the dealer, starting at his left, asks each player in turn how many cards he wishes to draw, up to three. Standard rules demand that players throw their discards in the center of the table, in turn. If a player discards two cards, he gets two more, and so on.

I have actually heard of players who say they can get four cards if they hold an Ace. I don't understand this option; why reveal even one of your cards to your opponents? Personally, I'd be torn—leave a game as soon as someone makes this foolish request, or stick around and help him leave the table lighter than he started. I guess it depends on how charitable I was feeling at the time.

After the draw, the betting is resumed, and when every player has either met the last raise or has folded, the remaining players show their hands and the high man takes the pot. After the draw is when the real poker begins, when your ability to read both cards and men comes into play.

For instance, if a man draws one card, he may be holding four to a straight or flush. But there is always the possibility that he has three of a kind and is holding a high "kicker," hoping for a full house. He might have two pair, sure enough, but he also could have four of a kind. Only your knowledge of your opponent and his style of play—and the odds, of course—can guide you through this pass without losing your scalp.

If the man is a plunger, chances are he is drawing to the straight or flush, or maybe even to an inside straight. In that case, if you have a good hand, either call or raise him, depending on what else has happened around the board.

I never fear a man who draws one card. The odds are that he is trying to fill a straight or flush. One look at the table in Chapter 10 will show you that this player doesn't have the percentages with him.

If you start the hand with a pair and draw three cards, and one of these new cards matches your pair, you have a very good chance against the man who draws one card. Of course, you can easily find out if he made his long shot. If he raises the original bet, by all means call him. If he just calls, raise him and test his strength.

Three of a kind is a pretty good hand in draw poker. With this hand it is wise to call all bets, unless there are several raises by men who have drawn only one or two cards. And, of course, that's where "civilized bushwhacking" comes in again. You must know whether the players who raise are inveterate fakers, solid players, or desperate plungers.

The rule in draw is that the man who opened is the first to bet after the draw. At this point, he has the privilege of checking, which means that he can pass without folding his hand.

Now, suppose he checks and another player bets. Has the original player, who checked, the right to raise the player who bet? According to Hoyle, of course, he has. But in lower-stakes games, many players think this practice, which is called "sandbagging," is first cousin to shooting a man in the back.

The vast majority of amateurs are against "sandbagging," but since I'm a professional, I'm for it. Here's why:

If I'm the opener, and I pass a good hand, I am trying to do two things. First, I want to discover who else has a good hand. Second, I want to get as many chips on the table as possible, in case my luck holds and I win. If someone then opens the pot, I must keep in mind how many cards he drew and what kind of player he is. Now whatever he is, but especially if he's a wild one, I deserve the same right to raise him that everyone else has. My caution should not be penalized while his bravado goes free.

The rule on "sandbagging" varies from game to game. It should be agreed upon by all players before the session starts.

There are other rules that require such agreements. For example, it often happens that no one has a pair of Jacks or better, and the deal passes around.

In this case, it is a common practice for everyone to ante again, and for the new dealer to call for

Queens or better to open. This is called "progessive openers." If this next deal fails to produce an opener, the next dealer will call for Kings or better, then Aces. If that fails to produce an opener, the deal goes down the ladder step by step to Jacks again. Often times, a dealer will call progessive openers and antes, which means the ante doubles every time a deal results in no opener.

After a few hands of this, all the players are steamed up. Without a card having been drawn, the pot is up to the ceiling and every player is tempted to stay in the hand even if all he has to draw to is an "Old Cat."

Now, this is really schoolboy stuff. It isn't real poker any more than mounting a hobby horse is real riding. It just *looks* like it, is all. What it is, is strictly a luck game. The dealer might as well turn all the cards face up, and play a round of showdown.

I like draw poker and I often play it in a dealer's choice game. But I only will deal it if I am way out in front—with a big stack of winning chips. In a situation like this I want to keep those chips. I will burn up as much time as possible by playing draw, which is about half as fast a game as stud.

There are some variations in the rules governing opening the pot in draw poker, but Jacks or better is the most popular. Players may decide among themselves that the pot may be opened on a bobtail straight—that is, a straight open at both ends—or on a four-flush. I have played in games where the pot could be opened with any pair at all, and also in the game called "guts," which means "open on anything—just so long as you have five cards."

One variation that builds a pot without any real skill is "pass and out," which requires that on the opening round of betting if you can't open when your turn comes, you must fold. This forces the player with good cards to open. But it is not pure poker. You can hang your strategy out to dry in games like these.

That goes double for the "blind-opening" game in which the first player is required to open the pot, regardless of the strength of his hand. Usually, the rules call for the next player either to double the opener's bet or fold, and so on around the table until all players who haven't folded have paid the freight.

This game may have been originated by a colony of impoverished prospectors awash with kickapoo juice. Maybe it is played for kicks in Eastern prep schools, but it just ain't poker.

There are thousands of players who don't agree with me, though, and they manage to have a lot of fun with these various forms of Comanche roulette.

They just don't know how much more fun they could have playing the real thing.

Let's get back to some of the standard rules of draw, which don't vary so wildly. Here are a few of the more important ones:

✤ Draw isn't played in games in which there are seven or more players. If six of the seven players ask for three cards, the dealer will run out. The dealer can, conceivably, collect the discards, shuffle them and deal out the necessary draw cards from this new deck, but this is often too time consuming and destroys the rhythm of a game and the concentration of the players.

✤ If the dealer exposes a card, the player must accept it until after the deal is complete. The card then must go into the discard and the player is dealt a new card. (Some authorities rule that the player has an option of keeping the exposed card or getting a new card right then and there.)

✤ If a player has been dealt six cards instead of five and has not looked at his hand, he should immediately call the dealer's attention to the mistake. If he does this fast enough, the next player to his left is entitled to the last card dealt him. If the man with six cards doesn't discover the error until after all cards are dealt and he picks up his hand, that hand is void. He is out of the play.

✦ If a player sees a card about to be dealt him and no one else sees it or can call it, he must take the card. Of course, this requires you to be fairly sure about the honesty of your opponents, often a risky assumption.

✦ In many high-stake games, players make a rule among themselves that a cut of the deck may be demanded and granted at any time during the deal. But this does not agree with the standard rules, which say that after the dealer has given each player five cards no player may touch the deck except the dealer, who is not allowed to cut. He must give each player what he asks for until all the draw requests are satisfied.

✦ If openers are required, the opener must show them after the winner of the pot has been determined. If he wishes to draw to a four-flush or straight, he may split his openers, but he must announce this fact and put the discard aside so that he can show his openers later.

There is another rule that should never vary: every player must deal the cards when his turn comes. If you see an old-timer pass the deal, you are entitled to view him with suspicion. It may sound real hard to say this, but there is the chance that this move is calculated to create the impression of honesty where it ain't. Pappy always said to watch out for the guy who passes the deal—and Pappy ought to know.

If I suspect that a dealer is cheating, I turn my hand down no matter how strong it is and watch this fellow like a hawk. If he wins, especially if there are three or four strong hands against him, my suspicion begins to grow like weeds in a cow pasture.

If this happens twice in a game in which this dealer has passed his turn from time to time, I assure you it doesn't happen again. The player is barred from the game forever—on penalty of exchanging his horse for a wooden rail.

There was one man I made an exception for in this business of passing the deal. That was my friend, Johnny Diebo, who was the best Indian scout I ever saw. He quit that dangerous business to work the medicine show route as a magician and shill.

Johnny, who neither drank nor smoked, whose nerves were like steel, and whose eyes were as sharp as an eagle's, could make a deck of cards do anything he wanted. I tested him many times, and each time he amazed me more.

No one who knew him would play with him, even if he agreed to pass the deal. Johnny could have made a fortune if he wanted to, but he was an honest Indian and, besides, he liked the way the tykes laughed when he traveled from town to town doing his tricks. He didn't want to let them down.

One night I ran into Johnny in Two Rivers, where I had some friends, but where Johnny was a stranger. I asked him to sit in our game.

I opened up a brand new deck of cards, shuffled them myself—double shuffle, French cut, and all.

I handed the deck to Johnny and said, "Now let's see you deal yourself a winning hand."

Johnny smiled and asked, "May I cut them myself?"

Everyone said, "Sure, go ahead."

Johnny did. In fact he cut them several times, and as he did he proceeded to lecture the players on the subject of how simple it was to deal a crooked hand.

When he had finished shuffling, Johnny called on the man to his right to cut. He dealt the hands out and you never saw such betting in your life.

When the cards were turned up, I held four Aces. Another player held four Kings, still another four Queens, still another had four Jacks. In fact, all players had four of a kind, except Johnny.

He had a straight flush!

Before the guns could be drawn, I let the others in on the secret.

Another time I asked Johnny to join a session. He agreed, on condition that he could bring Doc, who ran the medicine show, and that he wouldn't do any dealing.

The game went on for six hours. It was pretty lively, except that Johnny seemed bored to death.

When it was over, I cashed the chips. Doc had lost seventy-nine dollars, and Johnny had won seventy-nine on the nose.

"You see now," Johnny said. "This game is too easy for me."

"How did you do it?" I asked him.

"Very easy," he answered. "I watch each dealer shuffle cards. I can tell before he deals where most cards are."

Well, there was only one Johnny Diebo. But there are a lot of little Johnnies around, looking for a fast buck. So watch your step.

Chapter 6

How to Play Five-Card Stud

To me, five-card stud is the most scientific poker game of all. It has all the action any good player can ask for, and it puts your skill, courage, strategy, psychology, and patience to the stiffest tests the game can provide.

In stud, the dealer gives each player one card face down, and one up, before the betting starts. Another card is dealt to each remaining player after this round of betting, and another round of betting follows. This continues until each remaining player has five cards—one down and four open.

The one concealed card is the key to this game's fascination. Only *you* know what that card is. The four exposed cards may reveal the limitations of your hand, but they don't give the whole show away. The single missing factor may be the difference between a bust and a big winner.

If your hole card is an Ace or a King (as shown in this picture), and none of these cards show elsewhere on the board, by all means raise the opener on the first round. This does two things. If there are seven players, at least three with low cards probably will drop out of the pot, so you have improved your chances considerably. Then, if you are re-raised, you can be pretty sure that someone has a pair wired or

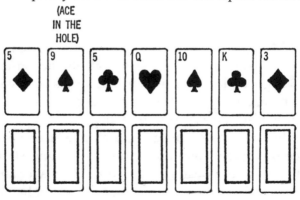

(ACE IN THE HOLE)

else is trying to force players out himself.

Either way, call or raise him again depending on how many players stay in. The more you raise and re-raise, the more players will drop out, and the greater your chances of winning.

There are a lot of variations to his play. For instance, if you have an Ace in the hole and a low card showing, and an opponent has an Ace (as shown in the next picture), your chances of catching another are slim. In such a case, I would drop out at once.

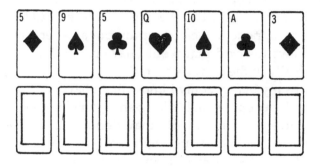

Now, suppose you get a low pair, back to back. Someone opens and the next man raises. You must scan the cards quickly to discover if the raiser's open card or yours shows elsewhere on the board. Then, if the raiser has a medium card showing, say, a Jack, and there are no other Jacks showing, you must figure that he has a pair of Jacks, with one concealed, or that he has an Ace in the hole. If I have, say, a pair of fives, and there are not other fives showing, I reraise, testing both his courage and his cards.

If he raises me back, then I can be reasonably sure that he has a higher pair than I, and I just call. In this way, I have accomplished two things. I have a fairly good idea of what the raiser holds, and I probably have driven all the weak hands out.

The dealer now gives each player who has stayed another card face up. If the original raiser pairs his first open card, then I know I'm beaten and I fold. But if, against all the odds, I draw a third five and my opponent doesn't improve, or another player draws the card that would have paired him up, I'm really in the driver's seat.

It's my bet and only I know that I have the high hand. If my opponent is a long-shot gambler, I check my three fives to him. He may decide that I have only a pair of fives (with a high card in the hole) and bet the limit—if he has a concealed pair that beats fives. If he does, I can read his hand almost as if all three cards were open and plot ways to get as many chips as possible into the pot.

At this point, I just call the bet, which is a cinch to confirm the fact that all I have is a pair of fives and a high card in the hole. He is going to feel pretty secure when his fourth card shows, no matter what it is. If this card pairs any one of his, except the first card showing, I know that I am still high man. The best he can have is two pairs.

With just one more card to be dealt, we are heading for pay dirt. I have a pair of fives showing and my opponent has a higher pair, so he must bet or check.

Nine times out of ten he'll bet, to find out for sure if I have three fives. Do I raise him, or just call?

If I raise I tip my hand at once. So I call reluctantly, hoping to convince him that I have a pair of fives or, at best, two pairs. I want to keep this pigeon in the pot, because I have him beaten and I crave his chips.

If my pigeon has two pairs, the odds against his making a full house are too big to worry me. So, after calling, I sit back to wait for the fifth card—and the kill. By this time, the raises have forced most of the other players to retire.

Now things can get *really* interesting. If my opponent draws a card that gives him two pairs up, I have to believe he has a full house. And, naturally, he'll bet the limit. If I have not improved, my normal play would be to call, just to keep the guy honest. That would be good poker.

But, if I know my opponent is a plunger, I will break all my own rules and raise him. If that doesn't let him know I have three fives, nothing will—though he still *might* read me for two pair. Unless he has a full house, his play is to call. Win or lose, this has been a battle for us both, the kind of battle that makes stud poker the game of games.

My standard rule in stud, as I've said before, is not to stay in any hand unless my hole card, or the one open card, equals or tops anything on the board. If I have a low card in the hole, and another showing, I immediately drop. I never forget the one most important rule of the game:

The player with the high cards has just as much chance to improve as anyone else. Since he has the high cards going, he has the best chance to win when all the cards are out.

Let's get back to the basic rules of five-card stud. After the dealer has dealt everyone one card face down and one face up, the player with the highest card showing must bet. The player to his left must call, raise, or fold, and so must each of the players in turn. After the fifth card is dealt the big betting begins, especially if there are two or more well-concealed strong hands.

When all bets and raises have been called, *every player who has stayed to the end must disclose his hole card to the other players, regardless of whether he won or lost.*

This rule has caused more brawls than any other in the game. But it's a fair one and should be followed in every game. Here's why:

Suppose two players have secretly made an agreement to split their winnings or losses at the

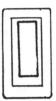

If you're hoping for a flush, this five-card stud hand doesn't look so good. But don't concentrate so hard on the flush that you forget other possibilities.

Here's a hand—exactly the same as the one above— that Bart tossed in thinking it was a busted flush. In the heat of battle, he overlooked that the club that broke his Ace-high flush was the King of clubs—he had inadvertently filled in an inside straight.

end of the session. In a deal like this, a player will raise when his partner raises, even though he knows that he himself has no chance of winning. That's how he builds up the pot, half of which he hopes will be his.

That's why when the hand is over, the callers

have a right to know what the other callers had in the hole. If a raiser who has lost turns up a low hole card and doesn't even have a pair, he is looking for a split lip for sure.

After each card is dealt, the dealer must call high man, who then bets or checks. After all bets are called, the deal goes on until the hand is complete.

There are a few other rules that tenderfeet ought to bone up on. For instance:

✦ If the dealer inadvertently turns a hole card up, the player who gets that card must accept it and take his second card face down.

✦ If a player, in disgust, turns his hole card up and demands another one down, the dealer should decline the request. Dealers don't often do this, but if they don't they are giving one man two chances at a high hole card, while the other players get only one chance. If a man doesn't like his hole card, he should turn his hand down.

✦ If the dealer skips a player while dealing the open cards, the players back the cards up until everyone has the card that belongs to him in the natural sequence.

✦ If cards are dealt before the previous round of betting is completed, the dealer must take back the cards dealt in error, then wait for the completion of the betting. Then he must remove as many cards from the top of the deck as there are players who have bet, and place them on the bottom of the deck.

Those are the fundamental rules of five-card stud. There are other "house rules," though, that should be agreed upon before the game starts.

The most important of these is probably that a player is responsible for calling his hand. The other players remaining in the hand are responsible for confirming that the hand is what the hand was called. A player may have a winning hand, but if he calls it wrong, once the chips are raked it's too late to correct himself.

Brother Bart was in a lively hand one night. He stayed to the end, trying desperately to fill an Ace-high flush. His first four cards were hearts, all high, and there were only one or two other hearts showing around the board, so he figured he had a fair chance to draw the fifth.

But the fifth card was a club. He almost folded the hand, but since the bet was checked around, he got a free ride, and thought that maybe an Ace-high hand could be a winner. After the round of checking, Bart turned his hand face up, and called that he had a busted Ace-high flush. Another player with two threes started to claim the pot.

The players around the board, knowing the rules, tried looking at the ceiling, at the floor, anywhere but at Bart—or the winner. I said nothing. After a few tense moments, the winner had finished raking in his chips. He knew he'd gotten a bit lucky because Bart, in his anxiety to draw the fifth heart, had completely overlooked the possibility of a straight. But he also knew that Bart was responsible for calling his own hand.

"You chump," I told him after the chips had been cleared. "Look at your hand again."

Bart looked, and his face dropped when he realized that he'd let his disappointment cloud his concentration.

Lying about your hole card, however, is not a crime in the game of stud poker. In this case, the cards talk—not the players. But how you make with the conversation has a lot to do with how you come out in the end.

For instance, if I draw an Ace on the first open card, I may say, "The pair of Aces opens," implying I also have an Ace in the hole. Perhaps I do have an Ace; no one knows except me. But when I make such a remark, I am counting on the other players to doubt me. Generally they do.

If one or two players happen to have paired their hole cards, I can count on at least one raise, and here's where I get smart. I just call and say, "So I haven't got Aces."

By this time I hope everyone is convinced that I don't have the Aces. If no pairs are showing after the next card is dealt, my play is to check the bet. My object is to force the man with a high concealed pair to open the betting. Almost invariably, he will. If enough players fold, I raise, and say something like, "I may not have Aces, but I have something just as good."

If the opener is a sharp player, or knows me, he'd fold, and not fall for my little play-acting. A decent player will call; if he is a plunger, he will raise. If he raises, I merely call him and wait for the kill on the last card.

If, on the last card, he still doesn't have a pair showing, I have the pot cinched. But I must know my man. If he is a plunger type, and I think he has a pair wired, I will check and hope he bets. The odds are that he will. If he does, I raise, and I have achieved what I started out for—to get as many chips as possible in the pot.

The danger in this strategy is that by keeping him in the game, I risk allowing him to get a second pair, or to get a third to match his pair. But that's why they call it gambling.

Conversation is an important part of any stud game. It helps to create the necessary illusion and confusion. But it should be confined to the game itself and not be allowed to roam all over the range. And if you've folded your hand, you've got no right to say anything until the next hand is dealt.

Chapter 7

Seven-Card Stud:
The Double-Action Game

Seven-card stud is, by all odds, the favorite of those who crave action, with chips piling sky-high in the middle of the table. The fact that three cards are dealt down, as compared with only one in the five-card game, throws science out the window.

In seven-card stud, the dealer gives each player two cards face down and one face up before the betting starts. In a game with antes, the player with the high card showing has the option of making an opening bet. If he checks, the option to open passes to the player to his immediate left. In a game with no ante, the lowest player on the table must open, if only for the agreed-upon minimum. If two players have identical low cards showing, the lowest card is determined by suit, in alphabetical order—clubs, diamonds, hearts, and spades—as I've previously noted.

After all the remaining players have either called or raised, and have met all the raises around the board, the dealer gives each of them one more card face up. At this point, the player with the highest hand showing has the option of making an opening bet. The same betting and dealing procedure is repeated until all the remaining players have seven cards, the last one of which is dealt face down. After this final down card is dealt, the high man on the board once again has the option of opening this final betting round.

After all the cards have been dealt and all the betting has been completed, the players who are still in the game select the best five cards from the seven they have been dealt. High hand among these is the winner.

In some games, a rule is made in advance that each player must select what he believes to be his best five cards and discard the other two. Under this rule, if he has miscalculated his hand he has no recourse. But it is becoming increasingly popular to rule that each player who has stayed to the end may turn up all seven cards, and that the best five cards actually constitute his hand. Even the best of players sometimes will fail to call his top hand.

But, as we've noted, in a high-stakes game, a player is responsible for calling his own hand correctly, to be confirmed by the other players. If he calls a lower hand than he has, it's his tough luck. In a game with a designated non-playing dealer, he will call all the hands and determine the winner.

This may sound a little complicated, but it really isn't. Here's how it works:

Suppose Player "A" draws two Kings face down and one up as the first three cards. He has a right to become enthusiastic about his chances. He has a bare chance to make the fourth King if none are showing on the board, and a good chance to make a full house, which even in seven-card stud is a very solid bet to win.

Let's say his next card is a nine. He checks the board, sees no pairs or Aces showing, and opens the betting. On the next round, Player "B" draws an Ace, and "A" a Queen. With no pairs in sight, "B" does the betting.

"A" now needs a nine or a Queen to make his

full house. Though he sees two other Queens showing and knows his chances of drawing the fourth are
very slim, he still calls all bets.

On the next round, "B" draws another Ace, giving him a pair in sight and high hand on the board.
"A" draws a ten-spot and his full house begins to
look doubtful. Still, a nine, a ten, or the case Queen
would turn the trick. He stays.

On the last round, face down, Player "A" draws
a Jack, which kills his hopes for a full house. In his
mind, it is now his three Kings against "B's" probable three Aces. The Aces bet and "A" reluctantly
calls, almost willing to let "B" have all the chips
without a fight.

At this point "B" reveals his third Ace and "A"
turns over his hand, convinced that his three Kings
have lost. Actually, his intense concentration on the
full-house possibility has made him overlook the
fact that he has a straight to the King—and a winner.
But unless "A" notices his mistake and corrects his
call to the straight before the player with triple Aces
claims his pot, he's literally out of luck. Another
player, of course, may point out the mistake, but this
is considered bad form.

This kind of thing happens so often in the best
of games that it is worth emphasizing. In a seven-
card game, you should take an inventory of your

hand after every card is dealt and check *all* the possibilities carefully.

As for strategy, my own rule is not to play for a fourth card unless my three first cards are high. These should include anything from three high cards without a pair, a pair and a kicker, or three cards to a flush or to an open-ended straight—or, of course, triplets.

Of all these combinations, the only really good one is three of a kind. To make winning hands out of the others is fairly tough, but if the betting isn't too rugged I will stay for another card.

If this card improves my hand and there are no threats showing, my play is to raise, hoping for a re-raise, thus eliminating as many players as possible. The other players don't know whether I'm raising on three of a kind or on pure guts, and their confusion helps me. Timid players will usually drop out of the hand, especially since I have a reputation for caution.

The element of chance in a seven-card game is tremendous. Over 40 percent of the cards dealt to each player, and as many as 60 percent of the best five, are hidden. It is possible to have a Queen and a nine showing, with no pairs or any other visible strength, and still come up with a full house with a pair of Queens and a nine in the hole. This is more

A harmless-looking hand, if I ever saw one. But it conceals a deadly combination, as shown below.

common than you think, which simply places more emphasis on seeing what cards have been exposed.

If you come up with a strong hand, well-concealed, your job is to get as many chips in the pot as you possibly can. This means that if the betting is weak, you must raise. But your strategy changes if two other players with good hands showing (but not as good as yours) begin to buck each other. In this spot, you just call each raise until one or the other of your opponents gives in. Then, if you have the chance, you make the final raise. Of course, you have to be darn sure you're holding the top hand at this point.

The possibilities for well-concealed winning

hands in seven-card stud are enormous. Three of a kind—a fairly good bet to win in this game—can be either completely concealed in the hole or partially concealed with a pair in the hole and one up. If the opposition is not too strong, you can win some nice pots with this combination.

No one can read your hand accurately. If you are lucky enough to have open cards that look like potential straights or flushes, your opponents will respect you more than they should. Of course, if the betting is heavy, you must be careful not to go too far with only three of a kind.

In seven-card stud, the principle of driving out as many players as possible, as fast as you can, should be applied with double force. If you doubt this, consider what happened to "Tick Tock" Davis, who for many years was the slickest seven-card stud man west of Independence.

Davis got his name because he would never enter a game without announcing the exact hour at which he intended to quit. He would lay a huge pocket watch down beside his chips so he could keep track of the time, and that watch ticked louder than any I ever heard.

The noise didn't seem to bother Davis any at all. But many is the time he drove losers near crazy by winding that timepiece a few clicks over and over again, or by checking the time with whatever clock was handy, or sometimes by just looking at that watch in the middle of a hand. It got so that Davis could get the players more interested in what time it was than in the hands they were holding, and this helped him in many a game.

The funny part was that if Davis was losing when the witching hour arrived, he would say, "Well, I guess I'll play along for another eighteen and a half minutes," or something like that. He would play along and most often he would at least come even, though sometimes it would take him the eighteen-and-a-half minutes plus a fifteen-minutes and a sixteen-minutes and an eleven-and-a-quarter minutes besides.

Davis told me this next story himself, and I'll try to give it to you in his own words:

"I'd been playing for six hours and seven minutes without winning a single pot that night in Dawson. I'd had a few fighting hands, but they always ended with me running second in a two-horse race. For the last three hours I had turned down every stud hand, and I don't think I had a card higher than a Jack in all that time. With the cards I had, I figured I couldn't draw water from a well.

"My quitting time was getting close, so when I got an Ace-ten down and the heart Ace up in a seven-card deal, I thought I had better make my move. I opened reasonably small, hoping to get some idea of where the power was. Only one player dropped and there were no raises.

"My next card was the ten of hearts, giving me two pair on the first four cards and two hearts showing, which was just dandy with me. The man at my left had a pair of eights and opened. When the bet reached me, I raised the limit. When this round was over, only three players were left: the eights, a King-four of different suits, and me, along with a hefty pot.

"With my raise they had to have me tabbed for a pair of Aces or better. Neither of them had four cards to a straight or flush, so I had to weigh whether they had two pair or three of a kind. Without any eights, Kings, or fours anywhere else around the board, I had damned little to go on.

"When they didn't bump me back, I ruled out any possibility of bluffing and figured that three of a kind was the least probable in either case. But they hadn't seen any other Aces or tens show up either, so they could have been holding back suspecting me of having triplets myself.

"With two hearts on top, I decided that if I got the breaks I was going to try to sell them that I had a flush going, and since I was the big loser, they might believe I was pressing out of desperation. If I didn't get the breaks, I was ready to bet or run, depending on how the cards fell.

"I got the Ace of clubs on the next round, which gave me an Aces-up full house in five cards, with just a pair of Aces open—the best hand I'd seen in six hours and sixteen minutes by the clock. The King got another four to make a pair, and the eights drew the case Ace. I was calling on the rainmakers to give at least one of my patsies a three of a kind. There wasn't any doubt in my mind that this was the big one that would bring me even before closing time.

"Here's how things stood: my Aces-up full house, which now was almost sure to be figured for three Aces, faced a pair of eights with an Ace on one side, and a pair of fours with a King on the other. I made a minimum wager to back up my Aces; had I not made any bet, everyone would have tagged me as a sandbagger and would have checked around. I was reasonably sure that one or the other of my opponents would call my moderate bet. Sure enough, the eights called, but the fours not only called but threw in a sizable raise.

"At first I thought to raise right back, but everything about the fours' raise told me he had it big, maybe even a full house. Two full houses in five cards is a pretty rare item, and since I had the big one, I wasn't going to let it go by without checking the fine points. I had to get all the chips I could into that pot before my time limit ran out. The boys just didn't like it when I stayed around for an extra twenty-one minutes or so to get even.

"I studied those fours for a long time, figuring that the longer I waited, the weaker my hand would look. If I raised back, I might as well draw him a picture of my full house. If I called, he would probably read me for three Aces at the most, or maybe the four-flush I was still hoping to sell if I was lucky enough to get another heart up. I couldn't figure a way to raise without tipping my full house, though maybe I might have kept him guessing about whether I was full of tens or Aces. Then if he had a full house, Kings up, he might get reckless, especially since the fellow with the eights had an Ace staring him in the face.

"If he had the full house at all, I knew he would stay whatever I did. But if he didn't have the full house, a raise might make him drop, and I needed his chips pretty bad. A call would keep him in regardless, and I'd have another chance on the next round. So I called. The eights folded, and it was just the pair of fours and me for the sixth card, with at least a couple of hundred bucks in the middle.

"On the next round, I got the best of all possible

breaks—the nine of hearts—and my opponent got the six of a strange suit. I bet fast, with the idea of clinching the notion that I had completed my flush and was now in command of the situation. The fours raised the limit. I hesitated, checked his cards, and then, as if I couldn't believe he had anything to beat my flush, I re-raised. This seemed to surprise him. But he was really hooked by this time, and he called.

"Fours didn't look happy when the last cards came around face down. I figured it this way: he had a Kings-up full house, and he had had me tabbed, just as I hoped he would, for either three Aces or for a heart flush. My re-raise had really rocked him, but the full impact of my strength hadn't reached him until just before he called. He could hardly fold his hand under the circumstances, but when he realized at last that he was facing an Aces-up full house, he was feeling just a little sick inside.

"I didn't even glance at my seventh card, but bet a fast ten dollars to give the impression that the flush was all I needed. He looked at his seventh card, though—and raised me! I had expected him to call, all right, or maybe—if he was made of steel—to fold. But the raise stunned me. I couldn't believe that I had sold the flush so well. I re-raised of course, and he bumped me again!

"At first, this had been more fun than I had had in a month of Sundays, but smoke signals were rising in the far reaches of my brain. This guy couldn't be that crazy, could he? Well, maybe he could, but I thought back around the table. Had there been any other fours opened? Well, if he had another pair of fours in the hole to match his open fours, there wasn't much I could do about it. So I just called him and, without waiting for him to show his hand, I flipped over my full house.

"But I never touched those chips. This hombre stood up and wrapped his arms around that pot faster than I ever hugged a lady. I knew then what had happened. He'd had a hidden Kings-up full house—he'd started with triple King right from the start—but the seventh card was a King, too. Four Kings he had, and three of them in the hole!

"From that time to this, I can tell you, I never let a sucker stay in long enough to draw a breath if I have him beat on the board. I could have had him out of there after the fifth card, when it was all mine. But, with six dry hours behind me, I got chip-greedy, and I let him draw out on me. That is midget poker, if I ever saw it. Here was a guy who needed four of a kind to beat me, and I let him stay around long enough to get 'em. I tell you, Bret, it took me fifty-five minutes and forty seconds to even things up, and I was real tired out when it was over!"

I believe that winning at five-card stud calls for seventy percent skill and thirty percent luck. In the seven-card game, the figures are probably reversed. Suckers for seven-card don't agree, but after playing thousands of hands in both games I think I'm pretty close.

A skillful player in seven-card stud pays special attention to his opponents' betting and to their style of play—maybe even more than he does to the cards they hold.

If the opening bettor on the first round has an Ace showing, and another man with a King showing raises the bet, I check the table. If there are no other Kings showing, I conclude that the raiser just *might* have a pair of Kings, or even three, with two of them in the hole. Now, suppose I have a pair of threes concealed and one showing. My play is to call the raise. From then on, I watch the betting and raising as much as I do the cards that fall.

If the raiser with the King up begins to show enthusiasm, I will take the possibility of his having three Kings more seriously. If someone else picks up an open King on the next card and my man still raises, I can be pretty darn sure that he has triplets, so I pack my bags and run.

However, if the raiser does *not* re-raise, I call, or

if I'm sitting on a barrel-full of chips I raise, just to test him a little. If I detect a reaction to my raise, which even the best of "poker faces" will sometimes reveal, I gear my play to it.

For example, if my opponent calls the raise with believable reluctance, I can assume that I have him whipped, and I turn my attention to the other hands on the board. Under these conditions, after the last card has been dealt, if the raiser merely checks or calls a bet made by another player, my play is to bet the limit, regardless of what my last card happens to be.

In doing this, I am hoping to convince everyone that I have three Kings beaten. If they're smart, they head for the hills. I do this even though I am reasonably sure that my man had only two Kings at the start, and either was hoping to improve or to drive the ribbon clerks out.

If he has two pairs he probably will call me. But if he really has three Kings he will raise me, in which case I must call him to keep him honest.

All this action is based on study of each other, rather than of the cards we hold. Since the three concealed cards remain a mystery, only our betting and our perception of character and motives will give any indication of our strength.

Figuring percentages in seven-card stud is tough

for the five-card player. Two pair in the first four cards for example, look awfully good, but the odds against making a full house out of them are still about five-to-one. They are worth a call, of course, but not against strong raising and re-raising. The play is to bet big off the bat and drive potential winners out of the game before they can draw triplets or better. If this doesn't work, drop. You're probably beaten already.

The same rules apply to four-flushes and possible straights on the first four card dealt. If you have four cards to a flush with three to come, the odds are less than even money that you will make the flush. This applies also to four-card open-end straights—with the odds against filling your hand increasing radically if the cards that fall one by one fail to help you. Thus a man betting a four-flush or four-card open-end straight on the first four cards is not exactly odds-on to come up with a winner, though many players foolishly think he is. How many times have you heard a player cry about not improving a flush on the first four cards? I've heard it a-plenty.

The same applies to an open-end four-card straight. Only eight cards in the entire deck will turn the trick, and with only twenty-four cards remaining to be dealt, the odds against making the straight are pretty big.

If I'm holding a four-flush or a four-card

straight, I never call. I either raise or fold. The raise will force weak hands to drop out and, if I am re-raised, I know where the strength lies.

After an hour of play in any poker game, you begin to get the "feel" of the game, and you learn to pace your play accordingly. You begin to sense who is strong and where the raises will come from. Sometimes this comes from conversation, sometimes from so-called poker instinct, sometimes from style of play or from sensing whether or not certain players are having a streak of luck.

Though I can't explain them scientifically, I have a few theories abut lucky streaks. One is that if a player wins two or three hands in a row, he begins to bet the limit or to raise all bets on every card. This, as I've noted, is respecting a streak.

This naturally intimidates players with weak hands and they drop out, leaving the "streak" player with little opposition. His chances of winning are thus increased.

But that's not the whole story. A player in a streak will tend to be so confident that he will call all bets up to the last card—and sometimes this will be the very card that makes him a winner.

In this way, the streak player can win with a bust against much better hands, especially if he bets strongly enough. It's illogical, but it happens.

The same idea works in reverse, of course. If you find yourself in a losing streak, the only solution is to turn down hand after hand, without betting a chip, until the cards begin to come your way.

Chapter 8

Hold 'Em: The Gambler's Game

If five-card stud is the most scientific game because only one card is kept hidden, what do you call a game in which everyone shares five of their seven cards? You probably call it loco. But in Las Vegas and among true professionals, the game is called hold 'em.

There are a number of Hold 'Em variations named for the states or cities that they were invented in, but the most popular form is called Texas Hold 'Em. This game combines the psychology of five-card stud with the nerve of five-card draw and may be the most demanding game in poker. It certainly isn't for the shy, the innocent, or the easily tempted.

Texas Hold 'Em is deceptively simple. Each player is dealt two down cards, then five cards are dealt face down in the middle of the table. There is a round of betting, starting with the player to the left of the dealer. This is called the blind bet or the "big blind"—which means that you are betting even though no one knows what anyone else is holding.

Since everyone has only two cards at this stage of the game, making a betting decision really separates the boys from the men.

After the round of betting, the first three cards in the middle of the table are turned face up—this is called "the flop"—which is followed by another round of betting. After this round, the fourth card is turned—called "fourth street"—followed by another round of betting, followed by "fifth street" or "the river"—the fifth card—and a final round of betting.

Everyone shares the five cards in the middle of the table. You make your hand out of one or two of your hole cards and as many cards as you need from the ones on the table. But in reality, the only cards you are betting on are your hole cards, which is where the fun begins.

The key to winning—or, more accurately, not losing your ranch—is your ability to resist temptation. If your first two cards are just interesting—say a five and a six to a small straight, or a couple of medium cards of the same suit toward a flush, you'll be tempted to stick around for the flop just to see an entire possible hand of five cards.

But don't be tempted. Mere possibilities in this game are like desert mirages. The more real that watering hole looks, the more elusive it eventually becomes. Medium cards are deadly in Hold 'Em, and sticking around will only cost you money.

For instance, you may be holding two medium spades, and you figure that's two-fifths of a flush. You'll stick around for the flop just to see if you can improve, which will cost you.

Two more spades then turn up on the flop, and that's four-fifths of a flush. You feel pretty good about your chances, and you'll call some more hefty bets.

Now you're around for fourth street. Your spade doesn't come up, but you're in this far and you have one more card to go, so you shell out some more green. Your palms start to sweat rivers as you call raise after raise, just to see the river.

But remember: the odds of getting a flush in a seven-card game still apply here. Actually, the odds are worse—essentially, you're actually hoping for three spades to be dealt in five cards, and those are

crazy odds. And, with two spades showing, everyone at the table not holding two spades will know
all those players staying around are only waiting for
fourth street and fifth street, hoping to see that fifth
spade.

Plus, anyone else with two spades in the hole
has the same chance as you of filling the flush, and
if they are holding the Ace or a higher card than
you, even a better chance.

This gives other players with more solid Hold
'Em hands—like a pair in the hole—a golden oppor-
tunity to raise like an angry bull. They know the
odds of you pulling that flush—they aren't good—
and will try to soak you for as much as you're
worth.

If you are dealt low cards, fold immediately,
even if they are of the same suit. Don't stay in hoping for a straight unless you have face cards that you
can match on the flop. In other words, stay in if you
have high cards. At least this way, you may get a
straight or a flush, or match one of your high cards
and end up with a high two pair or, even better,
three of a kind.

The bettor will always be the fellow with a pair
in the hole or a matched high pair on the flop. No
matter what cards get turned up on the flop, assume
that someone has paired up on the highest card

showing. For instance, if a Queen is turned on the flop, assume someone has paired up on his hole Queen, and so on. If you don't have at least a King in the hole, you are cooked.

An Ace in the hole, as always, is a powerful card, and should be used to drive other players out, especially if an Ace is turned on the flop—or even if it isn't.

One of the biggest pots I've ever seen in poker involved an Ace in the hole in Hold 'Em. The larcenous Commodore Devol held the Ace in his hole and, when the flop revealed no other Aces, he kept raising the limit until he drove out all the other potential pairs. Only one player remained, my brother Bart, who was holding on to a nine in the hole and paired up on the flop.

With no other higher cards showing, Bart could only hope Devol wasn't holding a higher pair hidden. Bart kept raising, trying to see if Devol was holding a higher pair. And Devol kept raising right back. Bart couldn't drop—he had the high hand showing. He was praying that a higher card didn't appear on board, or that he'd get a second pair or a third nine, and held on for dear life as fourth and fifth street revealed no higher cards to help Devol, but no other cards to aid his nines. No other Ace showed up, and Bart took the enormous pot with a pair of nines.

Some players craving more excitement stretch out the betting rounds in a Hold 'Em variation called Omaha, in which each common card is turned over individually, rather than the first three at one time. This creates more suspense and an extra two betting rounds. Players in higher stakes games don't like Omaha. It lengthens the game, for one thing, making it tougher for the house to collect its cut. It also keeps plungers in longer and minimizes the psychological aspects of the game.

To make this variation either more or less interesting, depending on your viewpoint, a seventh card is often dealt down to each player rather than up for everyone. Now everyone has three hole cards and four common cards, increasing the potential mystery.

Another silly Hold 'Em variation is called Mutual of Omaha, because it allows a player to buy an insurance card. A player can, for a pre-specified price, buy an additional down card after the seven cards have been dealt. A player with a four-card hand—two pair, straight or flush—has another chance of filling in his hand. But I think I'd stand a better chance of standing up to John Wesley Harding than surviving with my nerves—and life—intact after a game like this.

The Amarillo variation of Omaha Hold 'Em

forces the player to use both his hole cards to make
up his five-card hand. This restriction will eliminate
even more players before the betting gets interesting. A player with a King and, say, an eight of a different suit, might not be inclined to stick around for
long if another King doesn't turn up quickly, or an
Ace turns up, and the betting becomes frantic.

Chapter 9

High-Low Stud: Call of the Wild

I must devote a chapter to this strange game because it is becoming increasingly popular all over the country, even though no serious player plays it. All you need to win at this game is a fantastic amount of dumb luck, a large supply of guts—and lots of the long green in your money belt.

In this game of polite brutality, skill is almost no factor at all. However, a knowledge of certain fundamentals will reduce the number of bruises you receive.

The deal is the same as in seven-card stud, with no wild cards. When the seventh card is dealt face down the final betting begins, and it often leaves the table in a shambles.

There's a good reason. Unlike all other poker games, high-low stud provides for two winners—the man with the high hand and the man with the low hand.

In a seven-handed game, the battle of raises for high hand is precisely the same as in seven-card stud. But there usually are one or two players who think they have a chance for low, and they will raise the high hands again and again.

The possibilities of winning high hand, of course, are the same as in regular seven-card stud. The tricky hombre in this game is the man who is going for low. Assuming that house rules say that Ace counts as high only, it is easy to see that the lowest possible hand is two, three, four, five, and seven of assorted suits. But if the rules call for Ace being low as well as high, then Ace, deuce, three, four, six of assorted suits is the best low.

The topper is that one player can have both high and low hand, in which case he takes the entire pot himself. In this game of weird variations, that ain't hay.

Consider an example. Suppose you have, for low hand, an assortment of cards of different suits ranging from Ace to six. Examination of your three

Here's a combination that looks like a cinch for low. But it packs enough hidden power to take both high and low, as shown below. This is done by combining two sets of five cards each: the Ace, two, three, four, six for low; the five of diamonds for straight-flush high.

hole cards reveals that you also have a straight flush. In this case, using two different combinations of five cards out of the seven, you have top hands for both high and low and are practically a cinch to win it all.

Just be aware that a flush of all low cards is still a flush. For that reason, a low pair is not considered a "low" since any five disconnected cards will be lower.

After the last card is dealt, the rules call for bettors to declare whether they are going for high, low, or both. Each player does this in two ways, agreed upon before the hand; either in turn after the final round of betting, beginning with high hand on the board or by the last raiser, or by holding chips in their hands and revealing them simultaneously. In a chip declare, having no chips in your hand means you are betting low, holding one chip means you are betting high. Holding two chips means that you believe that, with differing combinations of five cards, you can win both.

More blood is shed in the betting that precedes this than in the Kansas City stockyards on a busy day. High or low, everyone tends to bet the limit—and the devil take the poor players caught in the crossfire!

After all bets have been called and the remaining players have declared for high, low, or both, everyone must turn up his hole cards. The best high and the best low hands split the pot—with odd chips going to the high hand. If a player has declared for both—and wins—he collects everything, of course, but he must win both the high and the low outright—no ties allowed. Ties for high split their half of the pot, and ditto for ties for low.

In this game, players with medium cards have

no chance whatever. They should fold after the first open card has been dealt without calling a bet. For instance, a player who draws a seven and nine in the hole and a Queen up has almost no chance for either high or low. He should run for cover before the lead starts flying.

The man with an eight-spot showing and two low cards in the hole, however, might have a bare chance of drawing two more low cards. These—if they don't pair him up—will give him a prayer to cop the low half of the pot.

After the first card is dealt face up, the action is between the high and low man. High man on the board bets first after each card. Naturally, the player who has a chance of making low hand will raise. Right then, all the other players can get a fair idea of who is playing for high and who for low. If the low player raises, the high player naturally raises back to force out the men in the middle, or to take their chips if they are foolish enough to stay.

From then on, it is a battle between high and low hands to get a maximum number of chips in the pot before the split. If all players drop out except the obvious high and low men, they both should check through the last cards and split the pot, unless one decides to go for both high and low.

But the game is rarely that simple. At least four

players usually bet up to the last card, and the action sometimes becomes so wild that all the chips in the game and not a few markers go into the pot.

High-low poker originated in the wails of players hopelessly caught in the toils of losing streaks. How often have you heard players cry, "I can't get a card higher than a ten-spot to save my life!" High-low was invented to ease their way to riches—or at least to give them an even chance. If luck ever stayed with one player consistently, this might make some sense. Since it doesn't, what's the point?

Still, high-low provides some solace for the Hardluck Harrys. If they lose, regardless, at least they have the satisfaction of going down fighting, with both guns blazing.

A point to remember, though, is that you can have just as much action in this game playing for pennies as you can playing for sawbucks. If you must bleed, it's better to bleed slowly than by the bucket.

One word of caution: unless there is a limit to the number of raises after each card is dealt, the game will deteriorate into either a slaughter of the innocent or a series of over-cautious strategems. Five raises on each card is more than enough to test the guts of any man alive, three is the custom.

The reason for this caution is obvious. Two players, with high and low hands, might reasonably raise each other until hell freezes over if they get a sucker in the middle willing to tag along with call bets. In the end, the sucker—unless he is struck by lightning—will pay dearly, and that's where this game becomes really brutal.

High-low stud may also be played with five cards. The rules are exactly the same as in seven-card stud, except there are only five cards dealt. This eliminates the possibility of going for both high and low, except in the almost impossible situation where—if Ace counts both high and low by house rules—an Ace-high hand wins high and an Ace, deuce, three, four, six takes low.

Five card high-low can get extremely confusing. An innocent-looking low hand may turn out to be a pair of Aces concealed, and a well-bet hand that looks like a high pair may turn out to be a low-winning bust.

There is much more science to this game than to the seven-card variety, because there is only one card concealed. Still, the player who is betting hard on the third or fourth card can draw a King on the last card to knock him out of the play. That is, if he hasn't been successful in driving the competition out.

In five-card stud high-low the player who reaches the fifth card with no pairs, no matter how high his cards, stands a good chance of winning low. He and the high man should be able to knock out most of the players in the middle.

This means, in simpler terms, that if you are really going for either high or low, you *must* bet the limit on each card dealt. If you are playing low, raise the high man, and vice versa.

The idiot son of the high-low poker family is called Lowball. Just is case some eccentric member of your group, who likes *you* to live dangerously, chooses this game, you ought to know how to handle yourself. In this game, low man wins all. The best thing to do if you get hog-tied in this situation is to quit if you get any card higher than a ten. Since any pair is almost certain death, perhaps the best thing to do is quit before the first card is dealt.

A hand of high-low, any way you play it, takes a long time with all the betting and raising, lingering decisions, and the splitting of the pot at the end. So whatever you gain in money-action, you are apt to lose in the actual number of hands completed.

Here's approximately how the various games break down:

Five-card stud—twenty-five hands per hour
Texas Hold 'Em—twenty-five hands per hour
Five-card draw—twenty hands per hour

Seven-card stud—twenty hands per hour
High-low, five cards—fifteen hands per hour
High-low, seven cards—ten hands per hour
With the house getting a cut on each hand, you can see why professional gamblers deal five-card stud or Hold 'Em. I have no doubt that the pros get as many as thirty-five hands an hour. Where there's a win, there's a way.

Big-time gamblers prefer five-card stud and Hold 'Em, too. They're in business, and time is money.

Chapter 10

The Deadly Mathematics of Poker

In a standard deck of fifty-two cards, with nothing wild, the law of averages—calculated by mathematicians who have tested thousands of hands—operates like clockwork, and that law can't be broken by even the highest authority in the land. It can't even be bent.

Talking now about five cards dealt to you with no cards drawn, the smart player, by studying this law, can estimate his chances when he picks up his hand. By doing so, he will learn to evaluate it against those of his opponents.

Statisticians have come to slightly differing conclusions about the odds, but all are close enough to leave no room for real argument. (One of the best authorities on the subject was a book published by the United States Playing Card Company, entitled *The Official Rules of Card Games, Hoyle Up to Date*. These tables were later updated by John Scarne in his book *Scarne on Cards* published by Crown. The tables in this chapter are used by permission of the respective publishers.)

A deck of cards contains an amazing number of possible hands, more hands than there are gopher holes, I wouldn't be surprised to hear. The statisticians, with their hair-trigger brains, have figured it out. Here are the possible poker hands in a fifty-two card deck:

Royal flushes	4
Straight flushes	36
Four of a kind	624
Full houses	3,744
Flushes	5,108
Straights	10,200
Three of a kind	54,912
Two pairs	123,552
One pair	1,098,240
No pairs	1,302,540
Total	2,598,960

The approximate odds against each combination in a five-card hand, as originally dealt to you with no cards drawn, are:

No pair	2 to 1
One pair	2½ to 1
Two pairs	21 to 1
Three of a kind	47 to 1
Straight	255 to 1
Flush	509 to 1
Full house	694 to 1
Four of a kind	4,200 to 1
Straight flush	72,200 to 1
Royal flush	650,000 to 1

It goes without saying that the royal flush is the prize catch. If you draw one in a five-card game, nothing wild, you will remember it for a lifetime.

In all my years of playing, I have drawn three: one in seven-card stud, the others in draw poker. In the latter two I only had to draw one card, and I would have been willing to settle for the straight or the flush. In all those years, I have seen no more than five other royal flushes. And luckily I wasn't betting into them.

Often, when there are not enough players in a game, someone will suggest that the twos, threes, and fours be removed from the deck, leaving forty cards. This is known as a stripped deck, and it auto-matically creates more action.

Here are the possible hands in such a stripped deck:

Straight flush	28
Four of a kind	360
Flush	980
Full house	2,160
Straight	7,140
Three of a kind	23,040
Two pairs	51,840
One pair	322,560
Less than one pair	249,900
Total	658,008

Now we come to the payoff—the table that must be studied by every poker player. It reveals the odds against improving any given hand in draw poker, when the rule is "Jacks or better" to open the pot.

The Deadly Mathematics of Poker

Cards held in hand	Cards drawn	Possible improvement	Odds against making
One pair	3	Two pair	5 to 1
		Three of a kind	8 to 1
		Full house	97 to 1
		Four of a kind	359 to 1
		Any improvement	$2\frac{1}{2}$ to 1
One pair with Ace kicker	2	Aces up	$7\frac{1}{2}$ to 1
		Another pair	17 to 1
		Three of a kind	12 to 1
		Full house	119 to 1
		Any improvement	3 to 1
Two pairs	1	Full house	11 to 1
		Any improvement	11 to 1
Three of a kind	2	Full house	$15\frac{1}{2}$ to 1
		Four of a kind	$22\frac{1}{2}$ to 1
		Any improvement	$8\frac{1}{2}$ to 1
Three of a kind and one odd card	2	Full house	$14\frac{1}{2}$ to 1
		Four of a kind	46 to 1
		Any improvement	11 to 1
Four-card straight, open ended	1	Straight	5 to 1
Four-card straight, one end or inside	1	Straight	11 to 1
Four-flush	1	Flush	$4\frac{1}{2}$ to 1
Four-straight flush, both ends open	1	Straight flush	$22\frac{1}{2}$ to 1
		Any improvement	2 to 1
Four-straight flush, one end or inside	1	Straight flush	46 to 1
		Any Improvement	3 to 1
One Ace	4	Pair of Aces	3 to 1
		Aces up two pair	14 to 1

A glance at these tables should be enough to convince you that you should never play poker loosely. If you do, the law of averages says you must come out a loser.

Among seasoned players, the man who "plays the percentage" may not be popular at all times, as I pointed out before. But he will wind up a winner, and that's the object of the game.

One example of playing the odds according to the percentages is in draw poker. Most players holding two pair discard one card in the hopes of filling in a full house. But this isn't always a good play.

Many players, based on the play and the betting, may believe that two of a kind won't be enough to win, and discard the lower pair! As you can see by the above table, the odds of filling in a full house when holding two pair are 11 to 1. But the odds of getting three of a kind when holding a pair are only 8 to 1.

While three of a kind isn't as good as a full house, it's a winner more often than not. Even the odds of getting a second pair, leaving you no worse than you were before, are only 5 to 1. If you don't get the second pair or the triplet, you can fold without investing any more cash in what was probably a losing hand to begin with.

If you can master the art of becoming a "percentage player," you will have the game more than half beaten already and will be the envy of other players who blow their bankrolls chasing flushes all night long. They may kid you about being a "tight" player, but don't forget that the guy who hollers loudest is usually a loser. All he wants is for you to change your style so he can get his money back.

The only way to make sure you know these percentages is to study them over till you can call them off in your sleep like the steps in a square dance. They are your ticket to fortune, and you can't get aboard the gravy train without 'em.

I use my knowledge of the percentages to make a little money on the side, winning bets in a game my Pappy has dubbed "Maverick Solitaire." As you know by now, the odds against a pat hand in a poker hand with five players are fairly high. The odds against two players out of five simultaneously drawing pat hands are a good deal higher, and the odds against all five players being dealt pat hands are astronomical. But I am always willing to bet that if you shuffle the cards and deal me twenty-five of them, enough for exactly five hands, I can arrange those twenty-five cards into five pat hands!

At first glance it looks impossible, but I've won a lot of money demonstrating that it isn't. As a matter of fact, it is almost impossible to be dealt twenty-five cards that *can't* be arranged into five pat hands. I figure the odds are at least 49 to 1 in my favor. Try it yourself. Only straights, flushes, and full houses count—no fours of a kind. If you can't do it nine times out of ten, you just aren't trying.

Chapter 11

Poker Etiquette:
A Lesson in Table Manners

The kind of poker you play determines your ethics and etiquette. To me, poker is a perfect demonstration of the every-man-for-himself principle, with no fair holds barred. Poker is played for real money. That takes it out of the class of pure entertainment and puts it on a par with, say, gambling on grain futures. When real money is at stake, I don't kid around. Do you?

Nevertheless, there *are* some rules. Only one of them is really important: *don't cheat.* Cheating angers men, or at least ruffles their feathers. Avoid disturbing your table mates in this manner. Anyway, cheating is against the law. Not only that, it's wrong.

The rules of the game take care of most other situations. Anything legal goes, provided all players are aware of what's happening. Sandbagging, for instance, is permissible so long as everybody knows it in advance. Ditto for betting a cinch hand.

Sandbagging

This is a "trap raise" device in which the opener, having a powerhouse, checks to encourage bets he intends to bump when his turn comes. There may be a bet and even a raise before the bet gets back to him, and when he raises, it's for blood.

Of course, the bet may be checked all around the table, too. This is one of the chances the sandbagger takes, but in such a situation he probably would not have gotten much play with an honest bet, either. So he can lay back and try sandbagging again on the next round—if his hand still looks good.

Some players consider sandbagging unethical, but actually it is the essence of good poker, which is to make the other guy think you have something that you haven't. When sandbagging is allowed, an opening checker is immediately tabbed for a possible powerhouse. If he raises, the suspicion is confirmed—unless he is bluffing, of course. This would be bluffing on a high level, but it still takes a man of courage to call such a raise.

Betting on a sure thing

Why not? You may play fifty years without holding a royal flush. When you get one, you had better use it. Properly played, it can make up for plenty of scalpings. That goes for any hand in which *you* know your opponent can't beat you—but *he* doesn't. Play the cards as they fall, and for all they're worth. If you can't do that—don't play poker. Certain circumstances may soften your heart from time to time, but to make it a habit is poker nonsense.

Playing out of turn

This goes unpunished in informal games, but it sure makes it tough on the other players. Checking, betting, or raising before your turn tips your hand and affects the play. Turning your cards down out of turn can help or hurt those that remain in the game. Your action will almost surely affect their betting, especially if they suspected you of holding a strong hand. Incidentally, after you have dropped, your cards are not available for inspection unless you have to show openers.

String Bet

This is calling and raising in two distinct motions, used by its practitioners to coax a reaction from the next bettor. The snake oil salesman who tries this will say "In call the $10 . . " then pauses and waits until he sees what the next man will do, then finishes the thought, " . . . and raise $10" if he sees the other fellow about to also call, or keeps his mouth shut if he sees a raise coming. The proper poker etiquette is to announce call and raise at one time, or announce the total amount of money being placed into the pot that indicates both call and raise.

A variation of this is done with bets made without the bettor announcing what the bet is. For instance, the varmint puts a $10 bill into the pot to call a $5 bet, but doesn't say anything. The next player then begins to call or raise what he believes is a $5 raise, when then our friend—who now knows his neighbors betting intentions—suddenly says, "oh, I want change from that $10, I only meant to call." Sometimes these mistakes are made out of innocence—but mostly not.

Rabbit-hunting

A dealer looking ahead in the deck to see what would have happened if he had stayed in the pot is strictly for kids. You will be tagged an amateur for sure if you do it.

Paying out the stakes

Poker operates best on a cash basis. Regardless of a man's credit rating, experience shows that lending money during a game is dangerous.

You can take checks, if you want to, for the original stack of chips. A player can buy more, by check, if it's all right with you.

But watch out, in any case. There's a peculiar quirk of human nature involved in this business. No decent guy is going to stick you with no-good paper, of course, but *every* poker player is inclined to be optimistic. He feels he is going to win. When he doesn't, he forgets that he issued the check on the expectation of winning—or at least of getting even. When the check bounces, he feels bad. But if you've cashed it, you feel worse.

He thinks of the deal as only a gambling debt. It isn't as if he'd stolen anything, is it? It was just a card game, wasn't it? And, of course, he'll make it good— sometime!

Professional gamblers, of course, have very effective ways of enforcing collection of bad debts. The average Joe in a friendly game hasn't.

Lending money during a game is just as foolish as cashing checks. I admit it's hard to turn down a request from a friend, but you'd better learn how. If you don't you may lose the cash—and your friend, too.

Chapter 12

Poker Cheats

Ever since poker began, men with larceny in their souls have used all sorts of ingenious devices to fleece their victims. Queer decks, marked cards, contraptions for concealing cards, and dozens of others are around a-plenty.

Marked decks, maybe the most popular of these, come in a variety of styles and are known as "readers." A trained eye can "read" these cards as well from the back as from the front, which can be quite a help in a poker game.

"Readers" reveal the face value and suit by small marks, sometimes in the upper left corner of the back, sometimes in the center. Other types have certain shading or variations in the thickness of the lines in the design. Much easier to read are the decks known professionally as "luminous readers." Large numbers on the backs become visible to wearers of special glasses, eye-shades, or visors.

Cheats who must play with strange decks use daubing material to mark the cards as they pass through their hands. Some crooks use a pin attached to the thumb with a small piece of tape with which they puncture the cards. Others use their fingernails to make indentations along the edges. A pin attached to a concealed part of their clothing also works well for these skunks. And there's a special wax for making the backs of Aces slippery, so a clever operator can cut them at will.

Some cheats bring their own decks, which is why it is always wise to insist on a sealed deck before play. One such queer deck is called a "sand tell" marked deck. This is a deck in which high cards are slightly sanded on the face, low cards on the back. When two sanded cards are flush, it's possible to deal two cards as one. For the shifty dealer, it's an easy chore to simply palm the unwanted card.

There are all kinds of "shiners"—mirror-like contrivances to fit on a ring, for example—that help crooked dealers read the cards as they come off.

Another cute item is the "concealer," which fits under the edge of the table and holds one or several cards until the dealer needs them.

One of the most intricate of these cheating contraptions is the Kepplinger Holdout, designed to be worn under the clothes. The Holdout is a series of pulleys and cords that hide a remarkable number of cards. By using his knees, a player can send cards down his sleeves into his hands at appropriate moments.

Yes, cheating at cards is a highly refined business, and there are a lot of men around who make money at it. In your own friendly game, you will probably never run into these varmints. But if you travel—take care. If one of these mail-order gamblers shows up in your game, you'll go home in a barrel for sure.

There is one type of cheating I am always glad to see. It's called the "spread," and is fairly common because it demands very little skill. Here's how it works:

It requires a team of two players. After each is dealt his hand, player "A" looks at his cards, lifts two fingers to his left ear, and rubs it in a most natural way. This tells his partner he holds, let us say, two tens. His partner, "B," has no tens, but he does have a pair of sevens. "B" raises two fingers and scratches the right side of his head, indicating the two sevens.

Player "A" reads the signal and glances at his hand. He has a seven, so he clears his throat in a most natural way and his partner goes on with the hand as if he had three sevens. Player "A" tosses his hand into the discard, but gently palms the seven with the face toward his palm. Player "B" tosses away three cards but calls for only two. The betting proceeds, the hands are called, and player "B" drops his hand with the cards bunched together and calls, "Three sevens."

"A" quickly leans forward, scowling fiercely and snarls, "Show your hand, friend!" He spreads the hand, revealing three sevens.

This routine can only be used a few times during any one session. I like to see it because a quick move can reveal "B's" four-card before "A" gets a chance to "spread" it into a winning five-card combination. I've won some sizable pots from the clumsy, small-time cheats who use this routine.

The care needed to protect yourself against poker cheats is also shown in the well-known story of the buffalo hunters. Flush from a big haul of hides, they got into a poker game with a professional gambler in Dodge City. The gambler, eager for an easy take, was willing to put up with almost anything, but the dirt and smell of the hunters rasped on his nerves. Worse, they played a cagey game, watching his every move so closely that he didn't dare palm a card.

As the pots grew bigger, one of the hunters shoved a wad of snoose up under his lip. A little later, he bit off a big chaw of tobacco. Finally, he lit a cigar.

The disgusted gambler saw a stream of brown juice trickle down the man's chin. "For God's sake," he snapped, "why don't you turn around and spit?"

The hide hunter stared back at him over the cards with beady eyes. "Not in this game, mister."

All of which leads to one conclusion: *never play with strangers.* One of them is likely to be the famous Stu Spofford, a slick character who could fast-talk his way into the president's office at four in the morning and sell him the state of Oklahoma. Stu served some time in the hoosegow, but always came out looking better than when he went in.

He even wrote some stuff for a paper once, telling exactly how he took his pigeons. He knew danged well when he wrote it that he wasn't going to hurt his trade. Because people are and always will be natural born fall guys, and Stu knew just how to make them fall.

I met Stu one day in the jail at Independence. He

was in not for bilking an innocent man out of a few thousand dollars; no, this master cardsharp was in for walking off in a pair of riding boots he hadn't paid for, believe it or not.

Maybe that proves that crime really doesn't pay. Because Stu had made nearly half a million cheating men at cards all over the West.

When I talked to him he didn't have a dime in his jeans. He even had to grub a cigarette. But we got to talking about things anyway, and I asked him, "Stu, how do you get strangers to play with you? Ain't they suspicious?"

"Wouldn't *you* play with me," he asked, "if you didn't know me, that is, and you were looking for a game?"

I had to admit I reckoned I would, for Stu looked like a gentleman, and a high-grade one at that.

"It's simple," he said. "I always sort of acted like a retired rancher who'd made his bankroll and quit ahead. I was travelin' for relaxation.

"I didn't have any trouble meetin' up with the rich men in whatever town I was in. I never started the games, but the subject would just sort of come up whenever I was around. Some wheel would suggest a game, and I would sort of agree to play for a while.

"In many games," Stu said, "I didn't have to cheat. I know enough about cards and averages to beat a sucker without doing a thing. But after lettin' the sucker win for a day or so, I generally turned on the heat."

Stu told me he practiced shuffling and dealing every day for hours, just to keep in trim. He was able to make the deck talk, almost.

Now Stu Spofford was one of the top men in his trade, but don't forget that there are lots of Stus around in every town, though they may not be as good. They're glad to take a hand in small games like yours.

These men are pure-bred actors. They hardly ever drink or even smoke. They have nerves of steel and smiles of pure gold.

They can con their way into two or three games a week, sometimes—big ones. They generally start out by playing a wide-open game, deliberately losing a few big hands. Then, when the suckers are ripe, they move in for the kill.

These characters come in all shapes and disguises. They tell the story of the pious-looking hombre who arrived in Tombstone one day wearing a black claw-hammer coat and clerical collar, and introduced himself as a minister of the Gospel. That night, to the surprise of the gambling fraternity, he turned up at the Oriental Saloon and asked if he could join a poker game. "Gentlemen," he explained, "I regard games of chance as God's means of favoring the elect and punishing sinners."

Invited to sit in, the preacher carefully hung his coat over the back of his chair and bowed his head in prayer for a short spell. Then he began to deal. Within two hours he had won most of the money at the table.

But one of the losers, becoming a mite suspicious, suddenly reached out and grabbed the preacher's wrist and pulled a card out of his sleeve. "Parson," the gambler said, "you better pray some more."

A dead silence spread over the house. The preacher rolled his eyes at the ceiling. "Brethren," he said, "let this be a lesson to us all. God works His will in wondrous ways. He has seen fit to conceal an Ace in my shirt. Glory be the name of the Lord. Amen."

The only time I heard of a clever cheat being beat at his own game by a tenderfoot was when Luke Simpson, the cardsharp, cleaned out a mild-looking stranger one night at a game in Laramie. The stranger seemed such an easy mark that Luke asked if he had any collateral so they could go on playing. "I got a stud horse outside," the stranger said. "Worth five hundred dollars."

Luke inspected the animal and agreed. But the stranger had a proposition. "I'll bet my stud against your stack," he said, "that I can cut any card in the deck you name."

"Any card?" Luke asked.

"You call it, I'll cut it."

Mentally drooling, Luke called for a fresh deck, shuffled three or four times, and slapped it face down on the table. "Jack of hearts," he said.

The stranger pulled out his Bowie knife and with one quick slice cut the whole deck in half. "If that Jack ain't in there somewhere," he announced, "I got a .45 that says I can find it."

Luke gave a sickly smile and allowed as how the stranger had won fair and square.

You may never meet one of these fellows, like I said. But if you do, I hope these words of advice help you to spot him. Since this is unlikely, I can only repeat the wisest poker axiom Pappy every preached:

"Don't never play with strangers. The fellers you know are trouble enough."

Chapter 13

How to Run a Poker Game

B y this time, you should know enough about
the wicked game of poker to hold your own
in any crowd. You *should*—but you don't. No
one ever does.

Poker is a game in which so many different
things are possible that you wonder whether anyone can ever get around to them all. Some people
will, and already have. But you won't until you've
got your feet good and wet in thousands of hands—
and even then the game has plenty of surprises.

To make your way smoother, though, here are a
few tips on how to run a friendly game with a minimum of ruckus and a maximum of pleasure.

BETTING LIMITS

Everything from penny ante to "no limit" goes in poker. Here are a few of the standard agreements:

Fixed Limit

A limit is set before the game begins. It dictates the amount of the opening bet and of the raises. Some players like the same limit all the way through a hand; others may want it increased as the hand reaches a climax—say, double after the draw or, in stud, double on the last card or after a pair shows.

Pot Limit

No player may raise more than the number of chips in the pot, this number to include as many chips as it may take to call the preceding bet. For example, if there are twenty chips in the pot and the bet is five chips, the player may put in his five chips to call the bet and then raise twenty-five. There can still be a fixed limit as to the size of the opening bet, the opening bet on each succeeding round, and even a top limit on the size of raises if the pot gets too big.

Table Stakes

In this game, no player may bet more chips than he has on the table. He may not remove chips from the table, nor may he cash any until the game is over.

He may purchase additional chips from the banker only between hands. This can be a very rough game, resulting in side pots as follows:

Suppose "A" has 500 chips; "B," 200; "C," 250; and "D," 300. "A" "taps out," meaning he bets all his chips. The amount of the following bets is determined by the number of chips owned by the low man (in this case, the 200 chips held by "B"). If "B," "C," and "D" want to call, they put in 200 chips each. This makes up the main pot, leaving "B" with no chips, "C" with 50 chips, and "D" with 100. "A" still has 300 chips to be covered.

The first side pot is made up of 50 from "C" and 50 from "D." "C's" chips are now exhausted, but "D" has 50 left. These go into a second side pot. Since there are no chips on the table to cover him further, "A" takes back his remaining 200 chips. From this point forward, "B," "C," and "D" may draw cards without betting.

At the showdown, if "A" has the high hand, he takes the main pot and both side pots. If "B" wins, he gets the main pot only, since he had no share of either side pot. If "C" wins, he takes the main pot and the first side pot only. If "D" comes out on top, he is entitled to the main pot and both side pots, since he has an investment in all three. High hand among the players having a share in each pot wins that pot.

When a player runs out of chips he can stay in the game, preserving his right to participate in the showdown and to win the main pot and whatever side pot he may have an interest in. If a player folds with chips in front of him, he is out, regardless of who holds the winning hand at the showdown.

Table stakes can be a blood game. For example, a player may "tap" another player, which means that he is betting the amount of chips held by that player. If he wins, he may clean the loser out completely. So don't play for these stakes unless you're really hot.

Whangdoodles

In a fixed-limit game, a round of Jackpots may be played and the limit doubled after somebody comes up with four of a kind or something else really substantial in the preceding round. At the end of this round, the game reverts to the original limit.

MECHANICS OF THE GAME
First Deal

By tradition, the first dealer is selected by dealing cards face up, one to a player. The one who gets the first Jack deals the first hand. The deal then goes to the left, clockwise.

Shuffle and Cut

The cards may be shuffled by any player, but by the dealer last. After the shuffle, the dealer offers the deck to the player on his right for the cut. This player may cut or not, but if he does not cut, any other player may. The cut must be at least five cards deep. If a card is exposed in the cut, the deck must be re-shuffled and re-cut. Following the cut, the deck must be put together and dealt as a unit. A re-shuffle or new cut cannot be requested during the deal.

Re-deal

A re-deal occurs:

1. When a deck is found to be incomplete or incorrect in any way. Money in the pot is returned to the bettors, but the results of the previous hand stand.

2. When it is discovered that the wrong dealer has dealt.

3. When two cards are found faced, or "boxed," in the deck.

Mis-deal

A mis-deal occurs:

1. In draw, if the dealer gives two cards face-up to the same player, and this player makes an immediate protest.

2. If the deck is not shuffled and cut, providing this is detected before the second round of cards.

Betting Interval

A betting interval is ended when the last bet is called. No player may raise himself. If all players fold but one, the remaining player takes the pot. As long as two or more remain, the deal continues to a showdown.

Improper betting

A player betting out of turn must, when his turn comes, make the same bet he announced unless:

1. An intervening bet calls for a larger bet on his part. In that case, he must either call or, if he wishes to fold after this raise, bet the amount that he announced, then fold.

2. An intervening bet smaller than his out-of-turn bet is made. He must then raise to the amount that he announced.

Passing out of turn dumps the offender from that hand. If he checked out of turn, a player must check when the bet comes to him unless an intervening bet is made. In that case, he may call but not raise.

The Showdown

Two or more players remaining in a game at the call are required to show their hands, although the losing hand may drop if he is not asked to show his cards. In case of a mis-call, the player must correct his mistake, without help, before the chips are racked. If a player mis-calls his hand higher than it actually is, only the remaining players in the hand or the dealer have the right to correct the error.

Opening for Jackpots

In this game, the opener must have Jacks or better. If he wins without being called, he must show openers. If he folds before the showdown, he must hold his cards to show openers. If a player opens without openers, and this is discovered during the course of the game, everyone gets his money back except that player and the game is void. The deal moves along. If the opener chooses to split his openers to facilitate his draw, he must announce it, and place his discard under the chips in the pot for inspection after the showdown.

Cards Exposed

During the deal, if a face-down card is exposed to the player about to receive it and it has been recognized by another, the player may demand a new one. The exposed card is buried in the deck.

Miscellaneous Regulations

1. In draw, the dealer must announce how many cards he is drawing.

2. No player may examine another's discards.

3. When dropping, a player must turn his cards face down on the table.

4. A player must protect his hand during the deal. If he fails to receive the proper number of cards, it is his own fault. If he is short, he must play with what he has. If he has too many, he may call attention to this before looking at the cards, in which event the dealer rectifies the error by taking the extra card and giving it to the proper player. If the player has picked up the extra card and looked at it, his hand is void.

5. Conversation is okay during a hand. But if you have folded, keep quiet. You don't know what you may say that helps or hurts a player still in the hand.

That's all there is to it. A few rules, a few tips, and a few suggestions, a few hard facts. The rest, as Pappy used to say, is in your hands.

Chapter 14

Other Wild Games:
Adventures in Pot Luck

An endless list of variations is roped together under the general heading of poker. Some of them are as far from the real thing as lead is from gold. Whether you play these games because you have more money than you know what to do with, or for fun (at very low prices), or because you have an irresistible craving for action, you must remember one thing: smile when you call them poker.

Sure, when the stakes don't matter, the game can be juiced up with fancy thrills and gimmicks.

Maybe regular stud and draw don't pack enough power under these conditions, so that luck can take the place of skill without anyone's getting hurt. But the experienced poker player can't take much pleasure in this. The best that can be said for these games is that they're better than being poked in the face with a sharp stick.

"Straights" Fowler, who beat Billy Dundee in the hand I told you about some time back, once got mixed up in a maverick game when he sentimentally turned up at his maiden aunt's engagement party in K.C. When the local dealers suggested a game, "Straights"—who'd been suffering through hours of small talk about schoolmarms and how to make punch—jumped to the bait quicker than the strike of a diamond-back.

When the ladies were asked to join, his hackles rose. He didn't panic, though. It was only when he found himself embroiled in games called "Up and Down the Ladder," "Pairs Wild," "Roll Your Own," and "Dirty Aces" that he realized what he'd gotten himself into.

Short of embarrassing his kindly old aunt, there was no way out. He went to pieces slowly, the wild games and the wilder chatter eating away his confidence and his bankroll. When it came his turn to deal, he called for five-card stud, but no one stayed.

"Let's play *poker*," the girls shrieked—and they called for a round of "Wild Willies."

As soon as he could, "Straights" headed west out of K.C. and to this day, as far as I know, hasn't been back. When his aunt invites him to come, he sends her money instead.

They don't play those K.C. variations anymore, but here are a few they do play.

Red Dog

Red Dog is a distant relation to the more modern game of Acey-deucy. Also known as Slippery Sam, Red Dog is a three-, four-, or five card game, usually played with a neutral dealer, neutral, of course, being a term open to interpretation.

A player bets a portion of the jackpot that the value of one of the cards he's been dealt will beat the value of a card of a similar suit turned from the top of the deck by the dealer.

For instance, I get dealt three cards, say, the King of spades, the seven of clubs, and the ten of diamonds. I can bet up to the total amount of money on the table that the first card off the deck will be a spade, club, or diamond and that my King, seven or ten will beat the value of whatever card the dealer turns up. If a heart is turned up, I lose. If a Jack of clubs is turned up, I lose. And so on. The game is pure gambling, as my Pappy pointed out, except when you're in cahoots with the dealer.

No Lookie or No Peek

This is as organized as a Chinese square dance. Seven cards are dealt face down. Nobody looks at the hands. The player to the left of the dealer turns up a card and bets. The next player turns up cards until he beats the preceding player on the board; he then starts the second round of betting. This continues with raises and re-raises until all the cards are turned up. This is just an elaborate form of showdown. There's more skill in a fast game of drop the handkerchief.

Razzle Dazzle

Here is a travesty of five-card stud. If your hole card is an Ace or a face card, the card that follows, and all of like value in your hand, are wild. This game is enough to unbreak a bronco.

Left to Right

Five cards are dealt to each player face down. Surprisingly enough, you can look at what you hold. You can replace one card, in turn, which you do unless you have a pat hand. Then the player to the left of the dealer turns up one card from his hand and bets. Others follow in sequence, revealing their cards in whatever order they choose and betting after each round.

This game is usually played high-low. I wouldn't play this game if I'd been drinking anything stronger than milk. On the other hand, maybe you need something stronger than that to get you to play it in the first place.

Front and Back

Seven cards are dealt to each player face down. Each player passes three cards to the individual on his right. Following this, each player passes two cards to the person on his left. Each player then discards two cards. The player on the left of the dealer starts the betting. High and low split the pot. (At this point, any poker players in the crowd blow their brains out.)

Four of a Kind

The dealer begins with one card all around, face up. This continues until a card appears that pairs anyone's open card. This card then goes to the player who has the matching card, and the player who would have gotten it in turn goes without.

Here's an example: if "A," gets a three, "B" a seven, and "C" a three, the second three goes to "A" and "C" gets no card at all. At this point, the betting begins, with the pair leading off or checking. Since this is a high-low game, and half the pot will go to the low hand, "A" is very likely to bet his threes, since he will get all subsequent threes.

On the next round, the dealer starts with the player whose card made the pair. This continues until someone get four of a kind, with bets intervening every time a card matches anything showing. Aces are low. Some people call it fun, but I think it is unconstitutional.

Frustration

This is two-card high-low. Each player gets one card down and one up. High open card bets. Another card is dealt around, face down. Each player discards one of his three, but always must have one up and down before the next betting round. High hand bets each time, and cards are dealt around and discarded in the same manner until each player has discarded two cards. Aces are high only. Straights and flushes don't count, just high pairs. High and low split the pot, while Bart and I join the Mexican army.

Dealer's Choice

Here the dealer names the game to be played.

Some limit this to the hand that he himself deals; others allow a dealer to call the game to be played all around the table. In either case, if not controlled, this game can deteriorate into a contest of absurdities. However, if the dealer is limited in his choice to the reasonable games such as five-card stud, seven-card stud, and Jackpots, you can't go wrong.

These are just a few of the brands of poker you may run into if you really look for them. If there is any doubt left about how I feel about these games, I'll spell it out for you. They are fun if you play for matchsticks with your maiden aunt's sister-in-law (fun for *her*, that is), but don't ever play this type of game for high stakes, or you may very well go home without your horse.

There is no end to the varieties of misbegotten poker games. The ingenuity of their inventors is equaled only by their persistence, with the result that even the following dillies, though they exhaust the players, do not exhaust the list.

STUD VARIATIONS
Five-Card Stud, Last Card Down

This is the same as regular five-card, except that a player may turn up his hole card and take his last card down.

Five-Card Stud with Replaced Card

After each player has received his fifth card, as in regular five-card, each can discard one card and receive another, as in draw. At the end of this round, another bet takes place. This is often played high-low, or for low only.

Mexican Five-Card Stud

Each player gets two cards face down. He decides which he will keep for a hole card. That hole card, and all of like denomination in his hand, are wild. He turns his other card up, and a round of betting follows. Each player then gets another card that he can either turn face up or use as his hole card, turning his original hole card up. After another round of betting, the process is repeated until each player has the customary four cards up and one down. The payoff is usually high-low.

Pistol or Hole-Card Stud

This is simply five-card stud with the betting starting with the hole card. This yields an extra round of betting—and more chips for the man who draws real lucky.

Six-Card Stud

The more popular way of playing this is with an

original deal of two cards down and one up. Each player gets three more open cards, and there are four rounds of betting. An alternative is to start with one hole card and one card up, with the last card dealt face down. This offers an extra round of betting.

Seven-Card Stud with Variations

Two cards are dealt to each player, one up and one down. After a round of betting, two more cards are dealt all around, one up and one down. There is another round of betting. Two more cards are dealt in the same way to each player for the third round of betting. The final card is dealt face down. Then each player discards one of his open cards and one of his concealed cards, retaining two exposed cards and three concealed. The remaining players bet the final round.

Three-Card Monte

The first card comes face down all around, followed by a bet. Two more cards are dealt, face up, with betting after each. The usual rating of hands applies, except that straights and flushes are made up of three cards only, and three of a kind beats either one.

VARIATIONS ON DRAW
Spit in the Ocean

Each player gets four cards face down. The next card goes face up in the center of the table. This card is regarded as the fifth card in each hand and is wild, as are all other cards of the same denomination in any hand. A round of betting follows. Then the players draw one or two to their four cards, as in draw poker.

A variation of this calls for three cards dealt face down in the center after each player has received his four cards down. The cards in the center are turned up, one at a time, followed in each case by a round of betting. Players may use any of the center cards combined with their four hole cards to make up a five-card hand. There is no draw and no cards are wild.

Cincinnati

Five cards are dealt to each player face down. Then five cards are placed face down in the center of the table. The center cards are turned up, one after the other, with betting after each card is up-turned. Players combine any of the center cards, as many as they choose, to make a five-card hand. No draw; nothing wild.

A variation, sometimes called Cincinnati Liz, is

played in the same way, except that one of the center cards is wild. It can be either the lowest card or the third card or the last card turned up—it's played all three ways. In either case, that card, and all of the same denomination in the hands, is wild.

Shotgun

This is a combination of stud and draw. Each player gets three cards down, and the players bet. Another card is dealt face down followed by a bet; then a fifth card, and a third bet. Then there is a draw and another bet. It is customary for the player nearest the dealer's left to open the betting each time.

Double-Barreled Shotgun

This is like regular Shotgun until the draw. Following the draw, each player turns up one card and the high card bets, as in stud. A second card is turned up all around and the high hand bets. A third and fourth card are dealt face up and two more bets occur, leaving one card face down. Then there is a final bet and the showdown. Cards must by turned up all at once at a signal from the dealer. Some play this game high-low; others choose to save their money for a rainy day.

Joker Poker

Add the joker to the pack as a wild card. This goes for any poker game, but it works out best for draw. In five-card stud, players wisely fold at the sight of the joker.

The Bug

Here the joker—called "The Bug"—is added to the pack and becomes a "restricted" wild card. It can be used as an Ace or as a wild card to complete a straight or a flush. This gets action in both draw and stud, since the sight of it does not always scare the opposition out.

Knock Poker

Each player antes one chip. Five cards are then dealt all around, as in draw. The balance of the deck is then placed in the center. The player at the dealer's left takes the top card and discards one. Players follow in turn, taking the top card or the last discard and discarding in turn. Any player may "knock" after drawing, and before discarding. He does so, of course, when he thinks he holds the winning hand. Then every player, except the knocker, gets one more draw and discards. Players may drop or stay. Each player who drops must pay the knocker one chip.

At this point there is a showdown for those who have stayed. If the knocker has the high hand, each player pays him two chips and then gets the antes besides. If another player beats the knocker, the knocker pays two chips to each player who stayed in, and the high hand takes the antes.

The game is also played without a final draw around the table following the knock. The pot in this case is composed only of the antes. Another variation calls for an ante of one chip every time a card is drawn.

The Wild Widow

Four cards are dealt face down to each player. Then one card is dealt face up in the center. A fifth card is dealt to the players. The center may not be used in any way, but all like it in the hands around the table are wild.

Wise Man's Poker

In this game, *all* the cards are wild. Only the dealer antes. The players don't wait for their cards, but fold in *advance* of the deal. After all the players have folded, the dealer picks up his ante and goes home. The other players follow. First one asleep in the bunkhouse wins.